CANADIAN HEALTHCARE FORMS AND POLICIES

Lorne Elkin Rozovsky, Q.C., F.C.L.M. (Hon.)
Member of the Nova Scotia Bar

CHIMA Canada's Health Information Team
Canadian Health Information Management Association
Canadian College of Health Information Management

LexisNexis®

Canadian Healthcare Forms and Policies
© LexisNexis Canada Inc. 2007
October 2007

Members of the LexisNexis Group worldwide

Canada	LexisNexis Canada Inc, 123 Commerce Valley Dr. E. Suite 700, MARKHAM, Ontario
Argentina	Abeledo Perrot, Jurisprudencia Argentina and Depalma, BUENOS AIRES
Australia	Butterworths, a Division of Reed International Books Australia Pty Ltd, CHATSWOOD, New South Wales
Austria	ARD Betriebsdienst and Verlag Orac, VIENNA
Chile	Publitecsa and Conosur Ltda, SANTIAGO DE CHILE
Czech Republic	Orac, sro, PRAGUE
France	Éditions du Juris-Classeur SA, PARIS
Hong Kong	Butterworths Asia (Hong Kong), HONG KONG
Hungary	Hvg Orac, BUDAPEST
India	Butterworths India, NEW DELHI
Ireland	Butterworths (Ireland) Ltd, DUBLIN
Italy	Giuffré, MILAN
Malaysia	Malayan Law Journal Sdn Bhd, KUALA LUMPUR
New Zealand	Butterworths of New Zealand, WELLINGTON
Poland	Wydawnictwa Prawnicze PWN, WARSAW
Singapore	Butterworths Asia, SINGAPORE
South Africa	Butterworth Publishers (Pty) Ltd, DURBAN
Switzerland	Stämpfli Verlag AG, BERNE
United Kingdom	Butterworths Tolley, a Division of Reed Elsevier (UK), LONDON, WC2A
USA	LexisNexis, DAYTON, Ohio

Library and Archives Canada Cataloguing in Publication

Rozovsky, Lorne Elkin, 1942-
    Canadian healthcare forms and policies / Lorne Rozovsky.

Includes index.
ISBN 978-0-433-44770-2

    1. Health services administration—Canada. 2. Health facilities--Risk management—Canada. 3. Health facilities—Risk management—Canada—Forms. 4. Medical policy—Canada. I. Title.

KE3646.R693 2007	362.1068	C2007-905796-9
KF3821.R693 2007		

Printed and bound in Canada.

This book is dedicated to my wife, Fay A. Rozovsky,
and our two sons, Joshua and Aaron

ABOUT THE AUTHOR

Lorne E. Rozovsky, Q.C., F.C.L.M. (Hon.) is a lawyer, author, educator and health management consultant. He has advised governments, corporations, and health agencies and associations throughout Canada, and in the United States and abroad. He has lectured in every province in Canada and in the Arctic, the U.S.A., Europe, the West Indies, Africa and Israel. He has appeared on national and local television and radio, and is the author of 18 books and over 600 articles. He was one of the first Canadians to be made an honorary fellow of the American College of Legal Medicine, and was the only non-American witness invited to appear before the Secretary's Commission on Medical Malpractice in the United States. He has served on the faculties of law, medicine and dentistry at Dalhousie University in Halifax, and is a member of the Nova Scotia Bar.

OTHER BOOKS BY THIS AUTHOR

Canadian Hospital Law; A Practical Guide (also in French as *Le Droit hospitalier au Canada: Guide pratique*) (Toronto: Canadian Hospital Assn., 1974)

Canadian Manual on Hospital By-Laws (Toronto: Canadian Hospital Assn., 1976) (with W.M. Dunlop)

Canadian Hospital Law, 2nd ed. (Ottawa: Canadian Hospital Assn., 1979)

The Canadian Patient's Book of Rights (Toronto: Doubleday Canada, 1980)

Legal Sex (Toronto: Doubleday Canada, 1982) (with Fay A. Rozovsky)

Canadian Health Facilities Law Guide (Don Mills, ON: CCH Canadian Ltd., 1983) (with Fay A. Rozovsky)

Canadian Law of Patient Records (Toronto: Butterworths, 1984) (with Fay A. Rozovsky)

Canadian Dental Law (Toronto: Butterworths, 1990)

The Canadian Law of Consent to Treatment (Toronto: Butterworths, 1990) (with Fay A. Rozovsky)

Canadian Health Information: A Legal and Risk Management Guide, 2nd ed. (Toronto: Butterworths, 1992) (with Fay A. Rozovsky)

AIDS and Canadian Law (Toronto: Butterworths, 1992) (with Fay A. Rozovsky)

Home Health Care Law: Liability and Risk Management (Boston: Little, Brown & Co., 1993) (with Fay A. Rozovsky)

Medical Staff Credentialing: A Practical Guide (Chicago: American Hospital Publishing, 1993) (with Fay A. Rozovsky and L.M. Harpster)

The Canadian Patient's Book of Rights (revd. and updated) (Toronto: Doubleday Canada, 1994)

The Canadian Law of Consent to Treatment, 2nd ed. (Toronto: Butterworths, 1997)

Canadian Health Information: A Practical Legal and Risk Management Guide, 3rd ed. (Markham, ON: Butterworths, 2002) (with Noela J. Inions) (foreword by Madam Justice E.I. Picard)

The Canadian Law of Consent to Treatment, 3rd ed. (Markham, ON: LexisNexis Butterworths, 2003)

PREFACE

This book was written as a result of many years of legal counselling and consulting to health institutions, organizations, associations and agencies in Canada. A significant part of this work was in the drafting of forms and policies and by-laws. In commencing work on any one of these projects, the first question to be asked is: Why? What is one trying to accomplish? The second is: How is this goal to be reached? To answer these questions, first a review is necessary of the organizational structure and of how the organization functions. Secondly, it is necessary to do a complete review of the law governing the organization.

Once all these questions have been answered and the decision made that a document of some sort is required, the major hurdle of writing the document must be faced. While one can start from scratch, the most efficient and effective way is to see what others have done. This does not mean that what others have done should be copied exactly, but one should at least learn from the experiences of others and then modify their documents to suit one's own unique practices, structures, goals and legal requirements.

This approach applies to everything from the drafting of legislation and regulations to policies to consent to treatment forms. The challenge is to get copies of these documents. Many through their own private networks, get in touch with as many people as they know and ask for copies. In some instances various organizations will publish prototype documents.

The purpose of this book is to provide a "network" of assorted prototype forms on a wide range of subjects, which can be used as the building blocks for the drafting of documents to specifically meet the needs of the health institution or organization that one is advising.

Over the years, the law, practices and attitudes change. What was an appropriate document some years ago, may not be now. For this reason, this book must be considered as a work in progress. Hopefully, there will be further editions with new prototype documents and changes in those that are found in the current edition.

To make certain that this collection, which is unique to Canada, is as current and as useful as it can possibly be, readers from across the country are invited to contact the publisher with suggestions on new forms that should be added, changes in any of the published forms, and any new forms that may have been developed. All of us in the health field may then benefit from everyone's experience.

Correspondence should be sent to:

Director, Product Development

LexisNexis Canada

123 Commerce Valley Drive East, Suite 700

Markham, ON, L3T 7W8

Canada

Tel: (905) 479-2665

Fax: (905) 479-2826

e-mail: productdevelopment@lexisnexis.ca

THE PURPOSE OF THE CD-ROM

Included in this book is a compact disc (CD) in the back cover. It contains a duplication of the material in both the policies and forms sections of the book.

The reason for the CD is purely practical. When a decision must be made as to whether a form is required or as to its contents, the CD enables the user to download the prototype document of interest, or to circulate it among those who should have input into the development of the document. Having the prototype in front of everyone so that they may make comments, additions or changes brings a certain amount of focus to the discussions, and results in everyone starting from the same foundation. It also means that everyone has the benefit of the prototype, and it encourages them to respond to each point in the prototype and to address the same issue in their discussion.

For the person doing the actual drafting, the CD can be used as a worksheet for the development of the user's own product. It must be recalled however, that these documents are prototypes and are not to be downloaded and used directly in the organizational process. They are to be used solely for the development of custom-designed documents that will fit the unique structure and policies of that organization.

CD-ROM INFORMATION

Introduction

The enclosed CD-ROM contains the text of the Forms and Policies from *Canadian Healthcare Forms and Policies* and is designed to be used in conjunction with that text. The text is in Word 2003 format.

Please note that there is no warranty, express or implied, that these documents are appropriate for the reader. Liability for the use, or misuse, of any documents is hereby waived.

System Requirements

The files on the enclosed CD-ROM have been designed for use on a personal computer with the following capabilities and configuration:

IBM or IBM-compatible with a hard drive and CD-ROM drive

Windows 95 or higher operating system

Microsoft Word for Windows 97 or higher software

At least 4.5 MB of hard disk space

Copying Files to Hard Drive

Before they can be used, files must be copied from the CD-ROM to a local hard drive or network drive. Create a folder (*e.g.*, "Canadian Healthcare Forms and Policies") on the drive into which you wish to copy the files. Open My Computer for a list of drives and folders to which you have access. Click on your CD-ROM drive. Select the Word files and copy to the Canadian Healthcare folder.

Retrieving, Saving and Printing a File

Files are accessed in the same way as any other Word file. Within Microsoft Word, select Open from the File menu, choose the drive and folder into which the files were copied, and then select the file you wish to open. If you make changes to the file, save the file under a new file name to preserve the text of the original file.

Depending on the application you are using, you may have different print options available to you. The type of printer you use will also have an effect on the final appearance of the text. Any style changes you elect to use may require adjustment or realignment to achieve desired page lengths or page layout.

TABLE OF CONTENTS

PART III — FORMS

Patients
Admissions/Assessments/Discharge/Exits

PART I

COMMENTARY

Chapter 1

PRINCIPLES OF PROTOTYPES

A.   THE PURPOSE

The provision of healthcare — regardless of how sophisticated or how routine — depends on four factors. These factors are the knowledge and ability of the person and the institution providing the care:

(i)   to determine relevant facts;

(ii)   to analyze those facts;

(iii) to decide what action must be taken on the basis of those facts and the analysis; and

(iv)   to take action according to reasonable standards depending on the circumstances.

This process may be more or less sophisticated or complicated depending on the discipline or profession of the provider and the task involved, and the facilities available. The provider may be a surgeon, a psychiatrist, a dentist, a physical therapist, a nurse, a dietician, an emergency medical technician, a homecare provider or any one of dozens of disciplines who provide care in hospitals, long-term care facilities, in the home, in emergency situations or in industrial settings.

However, with any profession or discipline, there are a large number of tasks that do not require this mental process. These are tasks that are either clerical or administrative. There is really no decision-making required, nor any analysis. They are simply tasks that must be performed when certain situations take place. These tasks may be part of the judgement process in providing care, and upon which the judgement process depends. The failure to carry out these tasks may jeopardize the care being given, cause injury to the recipient, and may be considered by the law as negligence resulting in a potential malpractice suit.

Once the situation arises in which professional standards dictate that a particular task must be carried out, it is no longer a question of the provider's judgement as to whether or not it is to be carried out. It may or may not even be a matter of judgement as to the manner in which it is carried out. There may be only one way to do it. In other words, no judgement is required. There is no professional decision-making involved except to recognize that such a situation exists, and then to do the task.

Similarly, there are situations in which certain questions must be asked to determine whether or not certain facts do or do not exist. Again, there is no decision-making involved as to whether or not this is done. The questions must be asked. The asking of these questions is required by current professional standards.

In theory, these clerical or administrative tasks must simply be done without thinking. It should be an automatic response that when certain conditions arise, certain tasks are carried out. The tasks themselves may require judgement skill, and the manner in which the tasks are carried out may be a matter of judgement, but the issue of whether or not to carry them out is not.

To put it another way, when certain conditions arise, certain decisions must be made. The question of whether or not to make those decisions is not an issue. It simply must be done as a matter of meeting standard practice requirements. Failure to make the decision regardless of what the decision is, resulting in patient injury, may be considered negligence or malpractice. The failure to address the issue and to make such a decision, or to ask certain questions, or to collect certain information, may be considered as a failure to meet ordinary, reasonable professional standards in the circumstances. This is quite apart from the conclusion of the decision itself. The result is that the failure may be considered negligence for which the provider of the care will be liable to the patient for compensation for any injury that results.

Because the focus of health professionals is on the assessment, analysis and decision-making process, these clerical and administrative tasks may be forgotten. The result is that part of the assessment or decision-making may not be completed, patient injury occurs, and a lawsuit and liability may result.

Much legal discussion and analysis takes place to determine whether or not there is liability for an injury. The object of risk management, however, is to attempt to prevent situations in which there might be a risk of patient injury or liability, or both, before it occurs.

Usually risk management concentrates on developing administrative procedures that will minimize or at least control the risk of a situation in which a legal obligation is not fulfilled and a lawsuit results. First of all, one has to design a risk management procedure that will assist in identifying those risks. It is then necessary to design a risk management solution which will control them. The purpose of forms and policies is exactly that.

(1) *Facilitate clerical and administrative tasks.* The first purpose behind the use of forms and policies is to concentrate on clerical or administrative tasks in the provision of services, so that health professionals do not have to remember to do them, or to remember to do all parts of them. It is to concentrate on tasks that do not require professional judgement. The purpose is to free the healthcare provider from clerical or administrative tasks, or to facilitate them in order to concentrate on the professional or judgement-making aspect of the provision of healthcare, which requires their training, ability and expertise.

(2) *Comply with required standards.* Since professional and institutional negligence involves the failure to abide by currently accepted standards, the challenge is to ensure that all professionals and employees know and follow those standards. It is common practice to provide, to encourage or even to require continuing education not only to remind healthcare providers of those standards but to instruct them on any changes in those standards, and to instruct them on how those standards apply to the particular circumstances of the institution or environment in which they are working. In-service education, grand rounds, communicating to staff of colleagues activities and changes or developments in institutional facilities and practices, and keeping abreast of current professional literature are all used to accomplish this goal. However, there is no systematized way of making certain that staff does this or that any of these methods will in fact affect or maintain required standards.

In many selected cases, predesigned forms may be developed along with policies requiring their completion, which may force an individual to follow required standards or practices that meet those standards. The advantage of the form in such cases is that it forces an individual to complete the form before the administrative structure of the institution allows a procedure to proceed. It also establishes a written record that required standards have been met.

The risk, however, is that the delivery of healthcare is to a very large extent a matter of professional judgement. Therefore attempts to customize professional conduct may have disastrous results when rules are followed to the detriment of the patient.

(3) *Improve communication.* A major cause of patient injury arises from the failure to communicate or the failure to communicate accurately. There may also be a failure to receive the communication or to understand it in the manner in which it was intended. The communication may be between numerous caregivers or other staff who have an effect on the provision of care, or between a caregiver and the patient, or the patient's family or representative.

This risk may be alleviated by training. However, since communication is a skill, some people have the ability to communicate more effectively than others. Some communicate more effectively and accurately in writing or electronically, whereas others are more skilled at communicating orally.

Predesigned forms can assist in managing this risk, by requiring as a matter of policy and procedure that in certain circumstances, certain specified information must be communicated to certain individuals in a certain manner and at certain times. The forms may be used to actually communicate the information, or to require that it took place according to the standards set out. It also provides a record that this has in fact been done, if the matter is later questioned in a lawsuit.

As in all other instances, predesigned forms have their limits. In many instances the communication of information goes beyond the quantitative, and is affected by the manner in which the comm-unication is given or even the circumstances in which it is conveyed. This would include for example, the tone of voice in which the communication is orally given, or through facial or bodily movements, which can change the communication of the words used. Rolling of the eyes, a shrug or a gesture, may totally alter the meaning of the communication, even a communication that is strictly governed by what is said and what words are to be used.

(4)   *Improve recording.* A further purpose of forms is to provide a means of recording that the person has in fact carried out the required clerical or administrative tasks, and as a result has, in at least that part of providing healthcare, met the legally required standards. It also provides a record that the required professional decision or judgement has been made — not necessarily correctly, but at least there is a record that the question has been addressed. This provides evidence that there was no negligence in failing to address required issues.

One could argue that a written record should be made for every professional decision. That would, at least in theory, provide the evidence required. However, that would require the provider to remember what to record and to record it correctly. A form eliminates this necessity. It tells the healthcare provider what to record and how to record it. It assists in improving standards of documentation, including compliance with statutes, regulations and professional standards, as well as internal requirements and policies that require certain information to be recorded, or to be recorded in a particular manner.

(5)   *Maintain consistency.* Prescribed forms also assist in maintaining consistency in the method of record-keeping by individual healthcare providers, throughout an institution, organization or agency, or even throughout a particular profession or discipline. This is important in risk management, since records that are not consistent with the usual practice may be seen as evidence of negligence in a lawsuit. In other words, they may be seen as failing to meet the generally accepted standard of care and, therefore, be considered as negligence in causing an injury to a patient.

(6)   *Remove dependence on memory.* A further purpose of having forms is to remove the dependence on the healthcare provider's memory to do what is required and to record it correctly in the required manner.

Thus, oral evidence by a witness in a court proceeding that a certain practice is that person's "usual" practice suggests that this was the practice that was followed.

The court may or may not believe this evidence based on the testimony of a witness, but there is always the doubt raised that perhaps the "usual" practice was not followed because it is based solely on the ability of the witness to remember correctly.

Considering the time lapse since the incident occurred, the vast number of patients that person has treated and the vast number of procedures that person has performed, it may be very questionable as to whether the witness's memory is accurate — even if it is. By having a written record made at the time, the evidence is much more likely to be believed, since it is more likely that a recording made at the time is more accurate than the memory of a witness. A form forces the provider to submit that evidence, and to submit it in a way that will be most effective as evidence for the defence.

If, of course, the form is not completed correctly, it will operate against the defence, as evidence that the appropriate practice was not, in fact, followed. However, even that can be helpful for any person or any institution sued. At least legal counsel will know what happened at the time, and can tailor the discussions towards an earlier and perhaps even more advantageous settlement.

B.   SOURCES OF FORMS AND POLICIES

Forms and policies may be designed by people in administrative positions, by consultants or they may be recommended by professional associations. The design and content of a form has three aspects. The first is legal. No form or policy should be implemented in any healthcare setting without first being reviewed by legal counsel.

Legal advice is needed for several reasons. The first is to make certain that nothing in the form or policy contravenes any prohibition in any statute or regulation, and that it conforms with any requirements that may be mandated. In an institution such as a hospital the forms and policies must also conform with any corporate or internal documents such as hospital bylaws or the mission statement. There must also be no conflict with any contractual obligations that the institution may have with other institutions, such as universities, or accrediting bodies, for example, the Canadian Council on Health Services Accreditation.

Another reason legal advice is necessary is to determine whether any liability could arise, not because of the contents, but by the way in which the form or policy is used.

The second aspect to consider when designing a form is risk management. The documents should be reviewed by the risk manager or by the person who is responsible for the risk management in the organization in which the documents are to be used. This will assist in determining whether the contents or the manner in which the forms or policies are actually implemented will create risks of liability or other risks, such as public relations problems. Such a review will also determine whether such a form or policy fits within all the other forms and policies used within the organization, so as not to cause conflicts or duplication.

Finally, any draft form or policy should be reviewed by the supervisor or administrator of any department or service that will be required to use it or be affected by it. It is absolutely essential that forms and policies not only do not interfere with the functioning of the clinical or administrative work, but will fit within the ordinary practice and procedure of providing care.

Professional associations frequently suggest various prototype forms and policies (see Chapter 3, "How to Use Prototypes"). These must be regarded as suggestions only, though they provide an excellent source from which to draw ideas for drafting these documents. However, they must be adapted to fit within the practicalities of individual institutions and healthcare providers. To do otherwise cannot only make them ineffective, but even harmful, with staff attempting to carry out administrative practices that contravene the actual practices or requirements of the site in which they are to be used.

Having said this, there are occasions in which current practices should be reviewed and possibly changed to fit within that suggested by associations.

A further source of forms and policies may be in provincial legislation and regulations. In these instances, the forms or policies may be required, in which case they cannot be adapted to local needs or practices. They must be used exactly as required. They either are included as part of a regulation, so that any alteration becomes a breach of the regulation, or the legislation may state that the forms will be in a format as required by another authority such as the Minister of Health. Reference must then be made to the forms which the Minister has designated, with those forms being followed precisely as if they were directly included in the legislation or regulations itself.

C.   THE RISK OF USING FORMS

While the use of forms has many advantages, in both preventing or at least minimizing the risks of errors and thereby injury and malpractice suits, as well as providing evidence for the defence of lawsuits, there are also certain risks in using standard forms.

These risks are:

1.   *The risk of an incorrect form being believed.* This may result in misinformation, relating to the facts, the times and dates, and the persons involved. The result will be that if in the course of a trial there is evidence by a witness that contradicts the information on the form, the form may prevail since it supposedly was made at the time the event being recorded took place, whereas witnesses must rely on their memories. which are always subject to question. Even, therefore, if the witness is correct, there is always the danger that the incorrect form will appear to be more credible than the live witness giving oral evidence.

2.   *The risk of a form not being believed.* If during a trial it is shown that there has been a general pattern of sloppiness in the completion of forms or in completing them accurately, the question can then be raised as to why this form should be believed. The result may be that the form that has been correctly completed may not be believed because, forms generally in the institution are frequently completed with errors. If this is the case, one may well ask how the court can accept the correctness of this form over a general pattern of incorrect recording.

3.   *The risk of not competing a form in a timely manner.* Just as in any other health or patient record, the failure to complete a form immediately after the event being recorded takes place, places the credibility of the information on the form into question. The issue can easily be raised as to whether the person recorded the information on

the form could have forgotten the information and therefore did not enter it correctly onto the form. This questionable credibility may seriously jeopardize the defence of a lawsuit brought against health providers.

4.   *Incorrect signatures.* Just as health records should be signed by an individual staff person, forms must also be signed by the person completing the information on the form and who has the knowledge to be able to complete it. Having other individuals complete a form also places the credibility of the form into jeopardy, especially if the person who signed the form testifies in court that the information is correct, or just does not know whether it is correct or not. Again, a further weakness in the defence based on this evidence occurs.

5.   *The failure to use a completed form correctly.* Many of the forms are not only valuable in themselves in order to complete or to replace the regular health record, but form a vital part of the system of risk management in the institution, clinic or office. Failure to use these forms as instructed so that they may be compiled with similar forms as part of a risk management profile, may jeopardize the risk management program to such an extent, that certain risks that should have been noted were not. The result may be injury, and potential liability.

6.   *The risk of not completing a form at all or omitting parts of the form.* All staff completing forms must adhere to a strict policy that all sections of forms must be completed. Failure to do this gives rise to the same suggestion as the failure to record certain information in any patient record. If it is not recorded that a certain event took place, and such a record is the usual practice, one can assume that without further evidence, it did not take place at all, even if it did. If a form seeks information that is not available, or not appropriate, the section of the form requiring this should note that fact. If the information is not available but will be available at a later time, a system must be established that will require automatic follow-up to insure that this information is obtained and added to the form. When this occurs, the addition should be dated as of the date on which it was added, and signed.

D.   THE DESIGN OF FORMS

In designing forms, a number of factors must be kept in mind. The first is that they must elicit the information required by law, by the risk management program, and by whatever is required clinically.

At the same time, the form must not contravene or require the person completing it to contravene any provincial, territorial or federal statutes or regulations. They must also not contravene any hospital or other internal institutional bylaws or policies. Nor must forms contravene, or elicit information that is contrary to, accepted professional standards, which would be used to judge the institution or any individual in any malpractice suit that may be brought.

If any of these factors change, the forms must be reviewed and possibly changed in order to maintain conformity. For this reason it is extremely important for any health provider or institution to keep its forms under review and to review all forms that may be affected by changes in legislation, internal bylaws or policies or professional standards.

Once changes are made in any form for any reason, all previous forms should be destroyed so that their inadvertent use will be avoided. So as not to confuse forms that are current with those that are out of date, all forms should carry a date of issue in small print in the same location preceded by the word "issued". The location and print style should be such that it will not be confused as being part of the form.

The wording of the form should not permit the reader to interpret what is being requested in more than one way. It must be absolutely clear as to what information is required in the various blanks. For this reason, anyone designing a form should pass it along to a person who is actually going to use it. The designer may have a clear understanding as to what information is required, but that is not necessarily what the person completing the form understands.

If there could be any ambiguity the form must contain very clear instructions as to how it is to be completed. For example, for dates, if the dates are to be recorded by numbers, the order in which those numbers are to appear must be specified, e.g., day, month, year or month, day, year. When names are requested, it should be clear as to whether the surname comes first or last. This is particularly important in avoiding confusion when a person has a first name and surname which could be confused. The term "Christian name" should not be used for a first name, since that term may not be used by non Christians, many of whom may not even be familiar with it. Similarly, the term "surname" should not be used, since there may be confusion as to its meaning. The terms "first name", "middle name" and "last name" are preferable.

If the form requires a signature, there should also be room for the name to be printed in block letters, with specific instructions requiring this.

The instructions on a form should be very specific requiring that it be completed using "BLOCK LETTERS". To make this absolutely clear, there should also be an instruction stating that additions are not to be in "cursive" or "writing".

Because of the risks of illegible insertions, even those printed in block letters, every effort should be made to keep handwritten insertions to a minimum. Wherever possible, check boxes should be used. However, because a checkmark is so easy to make, errors are also easy to make in checking a box or a space when that is not what is intended. To minimize this possibility, initials may be required instead of a checkmark, or a checkmark followed by initials. This two-step process hopefully will require a rethinking which will improve accuracy.

The designer of the form must think in terms of the form being compatible with the overall system. It is important, however, that those who use the form find it workable. It must be easily completed, easily understood and accurate in the information to be communicated, especially given the workload and time constraints of the individual service.

Quite apart from the actual contents of the form, the spaces and blanks which must be completed must be large enough and provide a sufficient amount of space to put in whatever is required, especially if it is to be completed by hand.

Because many of the errors that can occur are as a result of numbers (and this applies to health records generally), very clear instructions should be given at the beginning of the form as to how numbers are to be recorded. Problems invariably arise when there is more than one way to write a particular numeral. The way to solve it is to instruct the reader to write the number in a particular way. For example, the form should indicate whether a "one" is to be handwritten as i, 1, or I. This also applies to numerals "four, "seven", "nine" or "zero" .

Particular attention must be paid to the visual design of the form. Any spaces in which information is to be inserted must be big enough so that the words can be written sufficiently large and clear so as to be clearly legible. When boxes are used for check marks, they must be placed so that it is absolutely clear as to whether the box precedes or follows the instruction.

Since in many cases the person completing the form may have visual difficulties, the print font should be clear and large enough, with a sufficient amount of space between sections or sentences, so that they can be clearly seen by readers with less than perfect vision, including those with bifocals. Forms should be printed on flat white paper so that there is no reflection, and should not be printed over any design. Depending on how the forms are clipped together, the format should be such as to avoid any printing to be covered by clips on a clipboard, or removed by a hole punch.

If the forms are bilingual, a clear separation must be made between the two language versions, with the space on which entries are made or boxes are used for check-offs, being visually clear as to which instructions it relates.

Any instructions on the forms as to where the form is to be transferred must be clear, without any ambiguity, and placed in the same location of every form.

At regular intervals, the health information manager should review the design and content of every form used to ensure that the design is effective in carrying out its purpose, keeps errors to a minimum and properly fits within the entire system for information collection within the institution. The health information manager should have a regular practice of soliciting comments and collecting errors arising from forms, in order to monitor the effectiveness of the forms.

Chapter 2

THE USE OF FORMS AS RISK MANAGEMENT TOOLS

All healthcare providers run the risk of causing injury. There is also the risk of being held liable for interfering with a patient's legal rights, quite apart from any injury.

All healthcare personnel run these risks whether they work in an institution, in a group clinic or an agency, or as solo practitioners. Even if no injury occurs, or injury did not result from what health personnel did or did not do, there is always the risk of a lawsuit, of disciplinary action, of criminal prosecution, of bad press, or of damage to reputation. This is so in any profession whether it is law, social work or accounting. In healthcare, the risk is greater since the service being provided is so personal and often so intimate, that if it were not given with the patient's consent, it would be a serious interference with the patient's legal right not to be touched. It is this act of consent that changes the quality of the interference. That consent is given under very strict conditions, that is that the bodily interference will meet certain basic legal standards.

Because the bodily interference is so personal, the patient's emotional and psychological reaction to it may result in anger, fear, or disappointment, resulting in an attempt to punish the healthcare personnel who provided the care. These feelings may exist quite apart from whether the consent is legally binding or not. The result is legal consultation and potential action whether or not it is legally justified and whether or not a court will accept the allegations being made, which after all are framed by the lawyer acting on behalf of the patient.

Regardless of whether actual legal proceedings take place or not, and regardless of the result, no one ever really wins a lawsuit. The financial costs to obtain advice and prepare a defence can be daunting, even if these expenses are covered by insurance.

The mere threat of an action can have a detrimental effect on staff morale. It can ruin the reputation of individuals and institutions. This can affect the ability of institutions, academics, and individual researchers to obtain financial grants, the ability to attract staff, and it can affect relations with others in the field.

The preparation of a potential defence may involve a great deal of time, effort and money, taking away from the provision of healthcare and other activities that should take priority. The amount of time required of staff in an institution even during the initial discussions with defence counsel can be extremely disruptive. This price may be paid for years after the matter has died out, even if proceedings are dropped, or if allegations are proved to be false.

The legal task before all healthcare personnel is twofold. The first is to have tools in place to launch a potential defence in the future, but to do so without practising defensively so as to interfere with the provision of quality healthcare.

The second is to have an understanding of all the potential legal risks which might conceivably arise. This identification of potential risks must be an ongoing process. At no time should the excuse be used that since a particular risk has never happened before, it therefore can be ignored. There should be no satisfaction in knowing that there have never been any complaints about any particular practice. It may be that all is as it should be — or it may be luck. The fact that a healthcare provider or institution has never been sued, disciplined or prosecuted over a particular matter or practice does not mean that the risk of this happening does not exist.

The argument that quality care is provided does not in itself remove the risk of liability, or the risk that a lawsuit or a complaint of some sort will not occur, regardless of how lacking in substance it may be.

Motivation and good intentions also do not remove the risks. It is the failure to abide by legal obligations, whether under common law or in Quebec, civil law, or arising from statutes, regulations, bylaws, policies or contracts that gives rise to legal risks.

Having well-trained staff also does not totally remove the risk, though it is certainly a move in the right direction. There must be a system that is designed to manage the legal risks, that is, to either eliminate them, minimize their potentiality, or minimize the damage they can do.

The system that carries out this task of "controlling" the risks is that of risk management. Such a system must involve everyone in the health-care organization, whether they are health professionals, administrators at various levels, support personnel, board members or legal counsel.

In the past, the two terms, "risk management" and "preventive law" were frequently confused. In fact, there is a difference. Preventive law tries to determine what the risks are and what action can be taken in order to defend any legal fallout from those risks or what can be done to prevent or lessen the risks from arising. Risk management, however, is far broader. It explores not just the legal risks but the various risks that do not have legal consequences, but which have other consequences that are just as serious. Even more important is the fact that risk management tries to determine why the risk occurs, and tries to prevent it from occurring. The source of the risk may be strictly legal but often is social, cultural or administrative.

There is also a difference between risk management and quality assurance, with quality assurance relating almost exclusively to the subject of quality care of patients, residents or clients. Risk management is different because it goes far beyond quality care. While risk management programs attempt to maintain a certain standard of care, the focus is to identify the risks of liability and to manage or control them. This would include failure to maintain a certain standard of care, but would also focus on practices that do not necessarily relate to quality of care but do relate to potential liability.

The current interest in patient safety certainly falls within the umbrella of quality assurance, but it also does not have a specific focus on liability, even though liability may arise out of failures to maintain patient safety.

The purpose, therefore, of a risk management program is not solely to manage the risks of a successful lawsuit or complaint being brought, though that is certainly one of its objects. It is to manage the risks of being sued or being subject to some other proceedings such as a professional disciplinary action being brought even where it is groundless and will either be dismissed or discontinued.

Every risk management program consists of a number of steps:

1. *Identification of risks.* Do not assume that certain risks do or do not exist. Much depends on the nature of the practice and the nature of those being served. This first step applies not only to actual risks but also potential risks. The identification is performed both prospectively on the basis of experience elsewhere and on the knowledge of those involved as well as having input from the insurer for the service and legal counsel and, of course, the risk manager or the person who fulfils that function.

    Risks can also be identified retrospectively by the actual experience of past events at that facility or from incidents having the potentiality of a risk. To do this however, requires a system of recording these incidents, analyzing them and tracking them.

2. *Evaluation of risks.* Once risks have been identified, it is necessary to evaluate the risks in terms of severity and frequency. This is important in order to determine which risks should be given priority in terms of management. This of course, can only be done if there

are records of the risks that have either occurred or potentially could occur.

3.   *Elimination, reduction, prevention or minimization of risks.* If risks can be totally eliminated, and it is clinically and financially feasible to do so, it obviously should be done. If elimination is not possible, it may be feasible to reduce certain risks in terms of severity or frequency. Steps may also be taken to establish procedures that will not eliminate risks but prevent them from occurring. Finally, steps may be taken to minimize or lessen a risk from occurring where it cannot be either eliminated or prevented, but one can lessen the possibility of it occurring. Minimization includes preparedness to respond when specific risks arise, and the ability to take action when problems occur.

In establishing an effective risk management program where these various means are employed, records are vital in two ways. The first is to have records and a system of records that records the risks and enables them to be evaluated. The second is that once the risk management program is in place, policies, procedures and forms must be established in order to monitor the effectiveness of the program, and to require compliance with it.

In analyzing the facility from a risk management point of view, it is important to trace exactly what happens when a person has first contact with the facility, either by telephone, e-mail, mail or physically. Each step in the process must be recorded and broken down into its component parts: who has contact; what takes place in that contact; what records are made; what communications take place; and what actually happens to the patient. Once that list is established, it is then necessary to identify the risks that could potentially occur in each of the components. The next step as noted includes the analysis of each risk.

A response may then be sought for each risk. Since the response invariably involves a specific conduct or practice on the part of staff members, a determination must be made as to how that conduct or practice can be controlled. It may be that the establishment of a written policy is sufficient. In other cases, a written form which tends to require a certain conduct or practice may be the solution.

The reason that a form may be more effective than a policy, though the two may exist conjointly, is that the staff member who is required to act in a particular way is then obligated to record that the practice has been followed, whereas a policy on its own often does not do this. Forms tend to be most useful when specific procedures or practices must be followed rather than general conduct or approaches to situations.

The form has the additional advantage of being present before any practice or procedure takes place. It then serves as a reminder to follow certain steps as outlined in the form, and to make a record that these steps have been followed.

A further advantage of the form is that it specifies exactly what has to be done and in what order. As a record it provides exactly the form in which the record is to be made, so the potential error of not recording the correct information or all the information required is lessened.

Once the forms and policies have been established, not only must they be drafted following the advice of those who are actually going to use them, so that they are in fact workable, but the efficiency of the forms must be monitored. Constant attention must be paid to the issue of whether the forms are being completed properly, whether or not they interfere with the provision of care, and whether the purpose for which they are being completed is in fact being fulfilled. Regular legal and risk management review must be made, especially if either standards of practice change or whether the state of the law, internal bylaws, accreditation standards or contractual obligations change.

A review should also take place of any prototype forms or policies that may be used, such as those included in this book, to make certain that the prototypes are altered to fit the actual situation which exists. They should not be automatically adopted word for word without ascertaining that they do "fit". Changes made in them should only be done however, following the advice of the risk manager and legal counsel.

Once policies and forms are established it is vital that all staff are aware that they exist, know how to use them and understand their importance. This requires regular reminders not only for new staff, but for staff who may have encountered the forms and policies previously, but who may have forgotten them.

It is also important that staff do not develop an attitude that the forms are simply "clerical" and therefore do not mean very much. Careful supervision must exist to ensure that staff do follow the policies, and do complete the forms as required. Staff must also be made aware that their suggestions as to the efficiency and effectiveness of the forms are not only welcomed but expected. These suggestions must be recorded and staff made aware that their suggestions are being considered.

Chapter 3

HOW TO USE PROTOTYPES

The prototype forms, policies and procedures in this book are designed for the entire scope of health institutions, agencies, clinics and professionals and disciplines providing healthcare services. Each provider however, differs in scope and structure. While many of the issues that each face are similar, and in many instances may be the same, there are also very marked differences, even between providers of the same type. Not every long-term care institution is exactly the same, nor is every physiotherapy clinic, rehabilitation centre or community hospital.

In addition, the legislation both external and internal, and various other governing legal factors may be significantly different from provider to provider, and from service to service. This would include contractual obligations which exist, and any accreditation standards which may apply. The designation of departments, services, committees or positions may not be the same in the prototype as in the actual organization. In this book for example, designations are used, knowing that they will be replaced by the actual usage of the provider when its own documents are being drafted.

The usefulness of this book therefore, and prototypes in general, is on it being an idea bank from which one can draw when drafting forms, policies and procedures for individual services. It provides an idea bank of formats, wording and ideas upon which each specific service must draft its own forms, policies and procedures. The prototype also serves as a reminder that certain issues should be at least considered. It acts as a reminder of issues or items that need to be considered, accepted, rejected or altered.

In drafting documents of this sort and using prototypes as a basis, it is imperative to review the current structure and legal mechanisms which govern the health service currently. This must be done with the involvement of legal counsel; administrative officers whose authority would be affected by the implementation of the documents; and the risk manager.

It is quite possible that what will be drafted will be identical to the prototype, but that cannot be assumed. Each service provider must assess its own needs and circumstances to determine what must be included in its forms, policies and procedures.

With this in mind the prototype should be reviewed to determine how it can fulfil these requirements. On this basis forms can be drafted that will meet the needs and requirements of the individual healthcare provider.

A decision should also be made as to what forms, policies and procedures are even required. Not every organization works the same way.

In all cases, however, published prototypes should never be adopted word for word without such a review, unless for legal or other mandatory reasons, the provider is required to use a particular prototype without alteration, such as a prototype that is mandated by legislation or regulation. Even in that case, however, the prototype should still be reviewed. If, for whatever reason, the prototype conflicts with the requirements of the providing service, legal counsel should be consulted to determine how best to avoid such a conflict.

At no time should an item in a prototype that is not appropriate to the institution for which a form, policy or procedure is being drafted, be included.

The use of prototypes, however, are valuable when used in this manner. It is absolutely necessary to review the current structure and legal mechanisms which govern the health service for which one is drafting documents. This must be done with the involvement of legal counsel; administrative officers whose authority would be affected by the forms, policies or procedures in question; and the risk manager.

As with any prototype, no example in this book should be adopted without such a scrupulous review. Drafting can then take place on the basis of the prototype making such alterations as would suit the requirements of the individual healthcare provider.

With these cautions in mind, it is hoped that the prototypes will be useful in providing a basis for drafting, and provide ideas and suggestions which can be considered.

PART II

POLICIES

Policy 1.1: Standards of Conduct — General	
Objective:	*This institution depends on the co-operative effort and advice of both professional and community people. In contributing to the work of the organization, every individual bears a legal and ethical responsibility in the way in which they conduct themselves as part of the organization. Individuals in many instances may be held legally accountable for their actions as part of the board or any committee. Individuals therefore, cannot assume that responsibility remains solely with the group of which they are part or solely with the corporate body that owns the institution, though the institution may also be legally responsible.* *This policy is also designed to ensure that the institution maintains a reputation of honesty, fairness and professionalism in its dealings with the patients and every person with which the institution may have a relationship or potential relationship. As a matter of policy the institution must not only abide by its mission to operate in a manner for the best possible care of its patients, but also safeguard its assets, and not be influenced by factors based on financial or personal favours.* *In order to minimize the risk of liability, this policy shall be strictly enforced. Those individuals who may be in a position that would contravene this policy, should be prepared to resign from their positions on the internal organization or refrain from accepting positions in situations in which contravention is likely.*
Application:	*This policy applies to **all staff**, i.e., board members, members of medical staff committees and members of any other committee operating under the authority of the institution, all employees and volunteers.*
Cross-References:	P1.2.4; P2.1.2
Policies:	1. **Acceptance of money.** No staff member, volunteer, board or committee member, or any other person in the institutional organization shall accept any money or gift from any person in return for or in thanks for any action with respect to any service provided by the institution or any member of its staff, or for any action or any decision that has been taken by the institution or by anyone on behalf of the institution,

| | or for any promise that an effort will be made to undertake or influence such action. |
| | 2. **Commercial or financial interests**. No staff member, volunteer, board or committee member, or any other person in the institutional organization shall have any interest in any contract, or any corporation or partnership that has a contract with the institution, unless the details of that interest are made known to the board and are approved. |

Policy 1.2: Standards of Conduct — Board Members	
Objective:	*This institution depends on the co-operative effort and advice of both professional and community people. In contributing to the work of the organization, all individuals bear legal and ethical responsibilities in the ways in which they conduct themselves as part of the organization. Individuals in many instances may be held legally accountable for their actions as part of the board or any committee. Individuals, therefore, cannot assume that responsibility remains solely with the group of which they are part or solely with the corporate body that owns the institution, though the institution may also be legally responsible.* *This policy is also designed to ensure that the institution maintains a reputation of honesty, fairness and professionalism in its dealings with the patients and every person with which the institution may have a relationship or potential relationship. As a matter of policy the institution must not only abide by its mission to operate in a manner for the best possible care of its patients, but also safeguard its assets, and not be influenced by factors based on financial or personal favours.* *In order to minimize the risk of liability, this policy shall be strictly enforced. Those individuals who may be in a position that would contravene this policy, should be prepared to resign from their positions on the internal organization or refrain from accepting positions in situations in which contravention is likely.*
Application:	*This policy applies to all board members and members of any other committee operating under the authority of the institution.*
Cross-References:	P1.1; P2.1
Policies:	1. **Confidentiality.** Trustees and members of any committee shall maintain strict confidentiality regarding any discussion that takes place at their meetings, or any information which they learn either at those meetings or outside. 2. **Public statements.** No trustee or member of any committee shall make any public statements or give any interviews to the press on any matter relating to

the operations or policies of the institution except with the approval of the chair of the board.

3.   **Voting.** No trustee or member of any committee shall accept or agree to accept any payment or any property, nor agree to take any action, in return for voting in a particular manner, taking any position or taking any action in their role as a trustee or member.

4.   **Commercial or financial interests**

   a.   **Acceptance of money.** No board or committee member shall accept any money or gift from any person in return for or in thanks for any action with respect to any service provided by the institution or any member of its staff, or for any action or any decision that has been taken by the institution or by anyone on behalf of the institution, or for any promise that an effort will be made to undertake or influence such action.

   b.   **Contracts.** No board or committee member shall have any interest in any contract, or any corporation or partnership that has a contract with the institution, unless the details of that interest are made known to the board and are approved.

Policy 1.3: Standards of Conduct — Dress Code, Sanitary Deportment and Personal Conduct

Objective:	*The importance of this policy rests with the understanding that the origins of litigation against health professionals, institutions and organizations are frequently due to the failure to develop a positive relationship between patients and their families, and the healthcare staff. This does not mean that a good relationship will excuse patient injury, which may be considered as the result of negligence, However, it has a tendency to discourage litigation that may not be the result of negligence but is brought because negligence is suspected. A good relationship also makes the parties more susceptible to settlement short of going to court.* *While a good relationship certainly involves personal communication, understanding and empathy, it often begins with visual perceptions of the deportment, dress and general behaviour of the staff. While deportment and dress in a casual or relaxed manner may be acceptable to many, it may be regarded by some as offensive, or at least illustrative of a lack of interest and professional standards. If injury does occur, deportment and dress may be seen as evidence of lack of professional standards.*
Application:	*Reference in this policy to "staff" applies equally to medical staff, all employees, and volunteers. This policy is not to be regarded as all inclusive. Other policies may also govern staff deportment, conduct and dress. (See also Policy 2.3: General Administration — Volunteers)*
Cross-References:	P1.4; P1.5; P2.3; P3.1
Policies:	1. **Dress Code** a. Staff clothing shall be neat, clean, modest, appropriate for the environment and the work being performed, and shall not be sexually revealing or suggestive. b. Staff may be required by the executive director to wear specific clothing in designated circumstances. c. Staff shall not wear earrings or body piercings while on duty in the institution. d. No staff shall be employed who has excessive

tattooing on the face, arms, hands, legs or neck.

e. Buttons, insignia or clothing that carry any religious, political, social, trade union, professional assoc-iation or cultural message or slogan, other than the standard religious symbols, shall not be worn by staff without the specific approval of administration.

f. Jewelry, including watches worn by staff, is to be modest, discreet and shall not be of such a nature as to interfere with equipment, or the care of patients, nor shall such items contravene the accepted stan-dards of infection control.

g. Sandals with bare feet are not permitted.

h. No shoes or clothing shall be worn that may create a safety or infection hazard.

2.   Sanitary deportment

a. No staff member who suffers from any abrasion, lesion or any illness shall care for any patient without the specific approval of the occupational health supervisor, and shall have all abrasions, lesions or skin disorders covered, even if such cover is not medically required.

b. Staff shall not chew gum, or use tobacco or any non-medicinal drug or alcohol at any time while on the premises, nor be under the influence of drugs or alcohol while on the premises.

c. For personnel who smoke or use tobacco even outside of their working hours, the smell of the tobacco may remain on their person or clothing, which many patients may find objectionable and who may even be allergic to it. The absence of bodily odours on the part of personnel is essential.

d. Staff shall not wear perfume or highly perfumed deodorant or aftershave lotion. Some patients may find the smell objectionable and in some cases may be allergic to it.

3.   Personal conduct

a. No staff member shall use crude or socially unacce-ptable language or gestures in front of patients, their family, friends or representatives.

b.   No staff member shall express anger or engage in an argument with any patient, family or friend of any patient, or the representative of any patient.

c.   No staff member shall personally attempt to restrain any visitor who may be interfering with the care or treatment of a patient, or interfering or threatening staff or other visitors or patients, without immediately calling for security and the assistance of other staff, except when such action is urgently required.

Policy 1.4: Standards of Conduct — Relations Among Staff	
Objective:	*The purpose of this policy is to maintain a professional and collegial working atmosphere. This will allow each staff member to provide quality care, and to engender an atmosphere in which patients, their families and friends will have sufficient confidence in the ability of the institution and its staff to provide this care, so that they may contribute to the well-being of the patient.* *There will be situations in which there is a disagreement among physicians or between members of other disciplines, such as between two nurses, or between a nurse and a physician. This policy is designed to establish a procedure to solve those disagreements and to avoid patient injury that may result from such disagreements.* *It is also intended to prevent situations which would give rise to human rights violations, and constructive dismissal suits.*
Application:	*This policy applies to all members of the medical staff, and all employees and volunteers, students, faculty and any staff employed by outside contractors to the institution.*
Cross-References:	P1.3; P1.5; P2.3
Policies:	1. **Guiding principle.** All members of staff shall treat each other with courtesy, professionalism and dignity. 2. **Form of address** a. Staff shall address each other using their last names, except in those circumstances specifically permitted by designated administrative personnel, such as in the emergency department. b. For names that may be difficult for some to pronounce or are not pronounced according to English usage, the staff member shall be asked for the correct pronunciation. 3. **Inappropriate comments or actions** a. At no time shall the condition or appearance of any patient, or staff member, or trustee, or their religion, racial, national or ethnic origin, sex, sexual orientation or accent be commented on by any member of staff either on or off the

premises, both during working hours and at any other time, to any person, except in so far as the provision of healthcare requires such comment, nor shall any assumptions be made as a result of such matters.

b.   No staff member shall touch any other staff member or make any comments, remarks or gestures which may be taken by any reasonable person in either a sexual, threatening or harassing manner.

c.   No staff member shall threaten any other staff member with assault, nor any action intended to jeopardize the other staff member's professional, employment or social position.

d.   Staff shall refrain from telling jokes or distributing or displaying pictures, drawings, comments or other written material related to sexual, racial, political, or cultural matters, except where it is professionally appropriate for the care of patients.

e.   Staff members shall not criticize the work of other staff members in front of patients, their families or friends, or in front of other staff members.

f.   Any staff member who is responsible for caring and treating a patient who disagrees with any treatment order shall discuss that order with the individual who issued it, and seek confirmation, retraction or alteration of the order.

g.   Under ordinary circumstances no staff member shall unilaterally disregard, alter or otherwise contravene any care or treatment order given by another member of the staff regardless of discipline.

h.   If a staff member wishes to discuss an order under this policy with another staff member who issued the order and the staff member who issued the order is not available, the discussion shall be held with the supervisor of that staff member or in the case of a member of the medical staff, with the head of the member's department or the medical director.

		i.	In an emergency situation if the carrying out of an order is likely to cause immediate injury, a staff member who is authorized may retract or alter the order. This policy shall only be implemented if it would be unreasonable to consult with the person who gave the order, or such other person as required under this policy.
		j.	Any action taken under section 3.i of this policy shall be reported as quickly as possible to the supervisor or in the case of a member of the medical staff to the medical director.
		k.	Any action taken under this policy shall be recorded noting the reason for the action.
	4.	**Complaints.**	Any staff member having a complaint about any other staff member, if the matter cannot be resolved between them, shall pass on the complaint to the immediate supervisor or department head of the complainant. If a resolution is not forthcoming, the complainant may take the complaint to that person's immediate supervisor. If the complaint involves an immediate risk to the life or health of any person, or to property, the complaint may be made to the administrator on duty, or in extreme cases to security staff. All complaints shall be documented by the person receiving them with the advice of the complainant.

Policy 1.5: Standards of Conduct — Unacceptable and Disruptive Conduct	
Objective:	*The mission of the institution is to provide quality healthcare within its capabilities and resources. This requires co-operation, effective communication, courtesy and respect for co-workers, patients, their families and visitors. It is recognized that there will occasionally be disagreements. Allowing these disagreements or conduct to become unprofessional or discourteous has the potential of destroying the cohesive structure needed to carry out the mission. This policy is directed toward establishing a method of solving such disagreements. Failure to do this places patient safety and health at risk, and even the safety of staff and visitors.*
Application:	*All members of the medical staff, employees, volunteers, members of the board and committees.*
Cross-References:	P1.3.3; P1.4.3
Policies:	1. No staff member shall use crude or socially unacceptable language or gestures in front of patients, their family, friends or representatives.
	2. No staff member shall express anger or engage in an argument with any patient, family or friend of any patient, or the representative of any patient.
	3. No staff member shall personally attempt to restrain any visitor who may be interfering with the care or treatment of a patient, or interfering or threatening staff or other visitors or patients, without immediately calling for security and the assistance of other staff, except when such action is urgently required.
	4. Any conduct of any member of the staff that is disruptive in the operation of the institution or which places any other person or any property in jeopardy or at risk of injury or damage shall not be tolerated.
	5. Security officials and, if necessary, the police, shall be summoned to remove the person who is involved in disruptive conduct.
	6. The head of security shall investigate all incidents of disruptive behaviour and report the details of the investigation to the executive director.

| | 7. | All staff members who have been the cause of disruptive behaviour shall be subject to disciplinary proceedings, and in the case of members of the medical staff to the loss of medical staff privileges. |

Policy 1.6: Standards of Conduct — Oral Communications

Objective:	*The standards of patient care to a very large extent depend on the accuracy, timeliness and appropriateness of communications that take place among members of the staff of the institution or organization providing care. These communications are often oral, in which lack of clarity and misunderstanding can easily take place, resulting in patient injury. Because the communication is oral, there is no way in which to review the standards of the communication. As a result, the ability to communicate orally in an effective and appropriate manner is an integral part of the delivery of health care.*
	Quite apart from patient safety and the provision of appropriate care being provided as a result of oral staff communications, the risk of infringing a patient's other legal rights is also present.
	Failure to meet appropriate oral communication standards can also damage the professional atmosphere in which care is provided resulting in an aura of distrust, which itself can encourage unnecessary legal proceedings.
	This policy is designed to make staff aware of the importance of these standards and to develop as a matter of habit an ability to communicate in a way that will minimize these legal problems.
Application:	*This policy is designed to provide a constant reminder to all staff, including volunteers, to observe standards of oral communication and to be aware of the serious risks involved in the failure to meet those standards.*
Cross-References:	P2.3; P3.1; F13
Policies:	1. No oral communication intended for one individual shall be given orally to another individual with the request that it be passed along. Communications shall be given directly to the person intended if done orally. If this is not possible, written confirmation or other means shall be used to make certain that the communication is received.
	2. Every order or communication relating to the diagnosis, care or treatment of the patient must be recorded and clearly identified with the name of the person entering the information in the record.

3. Any person when speaking with patients, their families or friends, either directly or over the telephone, shall have the ability to speak and understand English (or French in a French-speaking institution or setting) in an accent and with fluency and clarity that is easily understood.

4. In speaking either directly or over the telephone, if there is any indication that the person to whom one is speaking is having difficulty comprehending, the call shall be referred to other personnel in an attempt to achieve understanding.

5. If the patient, or other person speaking with personnel cannot be understood, special attention must be paid to what the patient or person with the patient is trying to say. Be patient, but do not give the impression of understanding merely to be polite. If the communication difficulty is language based, make whatever efforts possible to obtain a translation. (See Form 13.) Without being condescending, repeat what the patient or other person has said explaining that you want to make certain that you understand correctly, pointing out that what they have to say is important.

6. If oral communication becomes particularly difficult, try to have someone who understands the patient be with the patient to help in understanding.

7. Discussions about patients or the care of patients shall not take place in public areas such as elevators or cafeterias.

8. Staff members shall never discuss the performance or activities of other staff members in front of patients, their families or friends or other staff members who are not involved, except where such discussion is professionally appropriate.

9. Personnel who have disagreements with other staff shall only discuss those disagreements privately or in the appropriate facility forum and, never in front of other staff members, patients, or visitors, except where such disagreements are matters before an appropriate committee or other administrative body.

Policy 2.1: General Administration — Board and Committee Meetings	
Objective:	*Over the last number of years, there has been increasing scrutiny over the practices and interests of members of governing boards of for-profit and not-for-profit organizations. The primary objective is that the organization as directed by its board of trustees carries out its mission as outlined in its incorporating documents, and the assets of the organization are protected. In addition, there is a duty for it to obey not only the general law and all applicable legislation, but all the provisions of its incorporating documents and its internal bylaws and policies.*
	This means that the members of the governing board have as their sole duty to carry out these objectives for the benefit of the organization, and not for their own personal gain or the personal gain of their friends or associates. For this reason the "conflict of interest" provisions of this policy are particularly important.
	It is also important that when the board or any other body or committee within the organization meets in order to carry out business, which is, in fact, the business of the organization as a whole, it conducts its affairs in the most efficient and effective manner possible.
Application:	*Everyone who is on any board or committee must be informed of this policy and have an in-depth understand as to how it is put into effect. It must also be agreed that any person who fails to meet the requirements of this policy shall be removed or resign from the board or committee.*
	In putting this policy into effect, it must be reviewed in light of application legislation, its incorporating documents and internal bylaws and regulations and drafted in such a way by legal counsel so that there are no conflicts arising between the various documents.
Cross-References:	P1.1; P1,2,4
Policies:	1. No person shall be a member of the board or any committee of the board if such a person is the spouse, sibling, parent, or child or business partner of any other person who is a member of the board, any committee of the board or the medical staff, or holds any office in the medical staff organization or

	any trade union with which the institution has a collective agreement.
	2. Any person on the board or who has an interest in any contract or in any corporation or partnership with which the institution has or is considering entering into a contractual relationship, shall divulge such interest to the board and shall not be present during any discussion of the issue before the board.
	3. All minutes, reports, correspondence and any other information, and the agenda for every meeting shall be given to each member of the board or committee at which such matters are to be discussed at least three days prior to the holding of the meeting.
	4. Members of the board and any committee shall be required to attend three-quarters of all meetings in any calendar year in order to maintain their membership on the board or committee.
	5. All procedure for all meetings of the board and of all committee shall be governed by *Procedures for Meetings & Organizations* by M.K. Kerr and H.W. King (Toronto: Carswell, 1996) or any later edition subject to the articles of incorporation and any bylaws made pursuant to it.
	6. All meetings of the board shall be closed to the public and the press except when a specific exception is made by resolution of the board. Committee meetings shall never be open to the public or the press. When the board by resolution allows the attendance of the public or the press, both may be excluded at any time during the meeting at the order of the chair, and shall be excluded when matters relating to personnel, members of the medical staff, patients, or any other matter identifying personal information of any individual.
	7. Institutional Review Boards: No member of an IRB who has any financial or professional interest in any matter brought before the IRB shall attend any meeting of the IRB at which such matter is discussed, nor shall discuss the issue with any other member of the IRB.

Policy 2.2: General Administration — Medical Staff Credentialling	
Objective:	*The purpose of this policy is to ensure that physicians and surgeons who are given privileges at the institution as members of the medical staff meet appropriate standards and form an integral part of the institutional staff.*
Application:	*This policy applies to all members of the medical staff and to those in administrative positions involved in the credentialling process, and to members of the board.*
Cross-References:	F37; F38; F39; F40
Policies:	1. No person shall be appointed to the medical staff unless the application for privileges includes the following: a. documented copies of educational qualifications; b. current licensure; c. professional association membership; d. proof of malpractice insurance; e. a statement of the licensing body in any jurisdiction in which the applicant holds a licence that no complaints are currently pending nor has the applicant been disciplined within the past five years; f. a criminal background check throughout Canada, and such other jurisdictions in which the applicant has either lived or practised; and g. documented evidence that the applicant is not suffering from either alcoholism or drug addiction. h. demonstration of spoken and written competence in communicating in and comprehension of English (or French in a French-speaking hospital) at a level and with an accent that clearly enables accurate communication with staff; patients; and friends, family and representatives of patients. 2. All applications to the medical staff shall be accompanied by a reference document in the proscribed form from the executive director of all institutions in which the applicant has practised, and that the document shall be verified by telephone by the chief executive officer.

	3.	All privileges given to any member of the medical staff shall be delineated in terms of scope of practice and procedures that will or will not be permitted.
	4.	Specific privileges will only be granted on the basis of the applicant's training to carry out the specific privileges granted, and on the basis of the ability of the institution to support those privileges.
	5.	Privileges will be granted only on condition of the applicant agreeing to enter into a contractual agreement with the institution to abide by its bylaws, rules and policies, and to undertake certain services that may be required by the institution.

Policy 2.3: General Administration — Volunteers	
Objective:	*As a matter of institutional philosophy, this institution shall endeavour to involve members of the community in its activities as volunteers. Volunteers are representing the institution when carrying out their work, and when appearing in public. These tasks may be seen as being carried out on behalf of the institution. Because these tasks could potentially cause injury, or damage to the reputation of the institution, its board and staff, it is possible that this might attract liability to the volunteers themselves and to the institution, This is true even though the volunteer is not paid. This policy is designed to protect the volunteers themselves, the organization, and the staff from both legal and reputational risks.*
Application:	*This policy shall apply to all persons designated as volunteers of the institution, and to members of external services, religious, community and other organizations, who wish to provide volunteer service to the institution.*
Cross-References:	P1.3; P1.4; P1.5; P1.6
Policies:	1. **Approval.** No person shall provide volunteer service to or at the institution without applying and being approved by the institution according to the procedure established.
	2. **Background check.** No person shall be appointed as a volunteer without a criminal background check of a nature and extent determined by the executive director, including members of external organizations when deemed appropriate by the executive director.
	3. **Educational programs.** All volunteers shall attend continuing education programs as to be determined by the professional standards committee.
	4. **Identity cards.** Volunteers shall wear an identity card at all times identifying them as volunteers.
	5. **Dress code.** Volunteers while performing volunteer service at or for the institution may be required by the director of volunteers to dress in a manner as determined by the director of volunteers, and may be required to refrain from the wearing of perfume or any article of clothing or jewelry which may

interfere with the care of patients, or otherwise create a safety hazard, or be regarded as offensive or create discomfort for patients, their families or friends. See Policy 1.3.

6.   **Authority of volunteers**

a.   No members of the medical staff nor employees shall give direction, orders or requests to volunteers unless volunteers have been authorized to carry out such orders.

b.   Volunteers shall not carry out requests by patients and refer those requests to employees, unless volunteers are specifically authorized by the director of volunteers to respond to such requests and have been trained to do so.

c.   The director of volunteers shall not give any authorization under this policy except when such authorization has been approved by the professional standards committee consisting of representatives from administration, the medical and nursing staffs, and the risk manager.

7.   **Relations with staff and patients**

a.   Volunteers shall treat all other volunteers, patients and their families and friends, members of the medical staff and institution employees and visitors with courtesy, kindness and consideration, and shall be regarded as representing the reputation and image of the institution.

b.   In any encounter with patients, families or friends of patients, medical staff or employees, volunteers shall clearly identify themselves as volunteers and shall not give any person the impression either directly or by implication, that they have any professional standing or expertise that may be used in the diagnosis, care or treatment of patients except as may be authorized by the director of volunteers.

c.   No volunteer shall touch any patient or be involved in any way in the care, diagnosis or treatment of any patient except when specifically authorized by the director of volunteers.

d. The director of volunteers shall not give any authorization under this policy except when such authorization has been approved by the professional standards committee consisting of representatives from administration, the medical and nursing staffs, and the risk manager.

e. Volunteers shall not at any time comment on the care, diagnosis or treatment of a patient to any patient, or their family or friends, nor shall volunteers give any recommendations regarding care, diagnosis or treatment.

f. Volunteers shall maintain and pursue the mission of the institution, and shall not under any circumstances treat any individual in the institution including any visitor to the institution, nor make any statement which may appear to discriminate or comment on an individuals' race, religion, national or ethnic origin, sex, physical appearance or mental ability, or sexual orientation.

8. **Confidentiality**

a. Volunteers shall not have access to patient nor personnel information or records either orally, through electronic means nor in writing.

b. Volunteers shall be required on being accepted to sign an oath of confidentiality not to divulge by any means any information with respect to patients, members of the medical staff, employees, or trustees, administrative staff, or any person or corporation involved in the work of the institution, or any information that volunteers may gain regarding any potential business or professional relationships that the institution may have or with any outside party.

9. **Complaints** Any complaints by volunteers regarding any matter shall be referred to the director of volunteers as quickly as is reasonable.

10. **Private promotion or solicitation**

a. No volunteer shall conduct, solicit or promote any private business while in the institution or working as a volunteer on institutional business.

b.   No volunteer nor any member of any external organization performing volunteer service for the institution shall promote any religious, political or social cause or ideology to any patient or their family or friends, or any other person while performing volunteer service at or for the institution.

11. **Injury report.** Volunteers shall report any injury, any potential threat of injury to themselves, or to any other person immediately to the director of volunteers or designee.

12. **Liability insurance.** Arrangements will be made that the liability insurance of the institution shall cover the activities of volunteers acting for the institution both on and off the premises, and any injury to volunteers, with such coverage being reviewed with the risk manager and the insurance committee on a regular basis.

13. **Public statements.** No volunteer shall make any statement to the press or public media relating to the institution or any without the specific approval of the director of volunteers following consultation with the executive director.

14. **Judicial testimony.** Any volunteer who is required by law to testify before any judicial body or who wishes voluntarily to testify before any governmental or legally authorized body shall seek the advice of the executive director before so doing.

Policy 2.4: General Administration — Theft	
Objective:	*This policy is designed to control and investigate the risk of theft by employees, members of the medical staff and volunteers. The theft may involve property of the institution, patients, other employees, members of the medical staff, members of the board or visitors. It includes but is not limited to, theft of drugs, paper records and information recorded electronically such as computer discs.* *While the investigation must be pursued vigorously, great care must be taken to prevent infringement of the legal rights of those being investigated, and to avoid infringement of employee rights under any collective agreement.* *While the investigation is proceeding, no information, statements or opinions relating to the specifics of the investigation or any identifying information are to be released or passed along to anyone including members of the board or any committee until the investigation is complete, except as permitted under this policy.*
Application:	*This policy applies to all employees, members of the medical staff, volunteers, patients and visitors.*
Cross-References:	P5.5
Policies:	1. When an allegation, complaint or report of a theft on the premises of the institution is received by the executive director, a specific file is to be opened on this matter, and to be maintained in strict safekeeping separate and apart from files on any other matter. 2. All details of the investigation are to be recorded so that a record is made that this policy has been met, including the name and signature of the person investigating along with the dates and times at which various elements in the investigation took place. 3. The investigation shall be under the direct control of the chief executive officer with the assistance of such other staff as the CEO may appoint. 4. Legal counsel shall be consulted so that the details of the investigation are part of a solicitor-client communication and therefore privileged. Advice

shall specifically be sought on avoiding a potential defamation suit against the employee, wrongful constructive dismissal, harassment, or a grievance under the collective agreement.

5. Any person under investigation who is called to a meeting to discuss the complaint shall be advised in advance that an allegation has been made, though no details are to be given. If the person is an employee who is a member of a bargaining unit of a union with which the institution has a collective agreement, the employee is to be advised that the union representative should be present, and shall also be invited. Any person under investigation who is not part of a collective bargaining agreement, shall have the option of having his or her supervisor or department head present, and if they so choose, legal counsel.

6. At any meeting under this policy the following advice shall be given:

   a. An allegation of theft has been made against the individual, though the source is not to be identified.

   b. The meeting is not a disciplinary hearing since currently nothing has been proven.

   c. The meeting is being held because the institution has a legal obligation to its patients and others to investigate allegations of theft.

   d. No public statements are being made by the institution and the allegations are not being held against the individual.

   e. The employee is under no obligation to answer the allegations without further thought and consultation.

   f. To protect everyone a record is being made of the allegations and the meeting, but as long as the allegations are not proven they will not be held against the employee, and the record will state that the allegations are unproven.

7. The individual under investigation shall be asked whether he or she has any further information or thoughts which would clarify the allegation.

| | 8. | The individual shall be informed that it may be necessary to transfer him or her to a different position or location, as long as the allegations are unproven, but that such a transfer will not affect the individual's seniority. |
| | 9. | The individual shall be informed that his or her conduct will be monitored both for his or her own protection and that of the institution, if the allegations are found to be false. |

Policy 3.1: Patient Relations — Staff Communication with Patients

Objective:	At one time, extreme care was taken in hospitals and doctors' offices to ensure what was referred to as the modesty of the patient. This involved very strict nursing procedures with respect to the draping of patients, and taking precautions so that no patient would feel embarrassed. For this reason, perhaps more than any other, male physicians were careful not to be alone with a female patient who may be disrobed or who may be undergoing a physical examination.
	In the last few years however, much more public attention has been paid not so much to patients' feelings of modesty and dignity, though perhaps it should be, but instead to the risk to the physician or other health personnel that the patient may make an accusation of sexual impropriety, or even assault.
	Despite the impression that society is more relaxed and informal than it once was, the reality is that not everyone in society feels that way. Health personnel who may be very comfortable with the sight of the most intimate features of human anatomy should not assume that every patient is equally at ease. Similarly, assumptions should not be made about a person's feelings based on age, sex, occupation or any other extraneous factor.
	Regardless of whether or not health personnel have met appropriate legal standards, the commencement of legal proceedings or of a complaint frequently arises on the basis of whether the patient liked the health provider or felt abused or insulted. A patient may have felt that insufficient respect was given simply by the unspoken conduct of the health personnel.
	Oral communications are frequently misunderstood, incorrect, misinterpreted or forgotten. The result may be patient injury and subsequent liability. This policy is designed to minimize the risk of this happening.
	The issue of rejecting staff on the basis of foreign or domestic accents may be seen as a risk management issue, because of the potential risk of an allegation of discrimination under provincial or territorial human rights legislation. It must be made very clear therefore, that there will be no discrimination contrary to law. The hiring of individuals whose ability to speak the language

	of the facility and to speak it in an accent that is clearly understandable, especially by the elderly, or hard of hearing, may be a prerequisite for many positions. Failure to have employees or medical staffs who do not have linguistic fluency may result in patient injury and risk liability. *The same is true with respect to an employee's or medical staff member's language comprehension, and equally applies with the ability to speak and understand required foreign languages. The policy applies equally to the ability to write in a clear and legible manner. Communicating in a comprehensible manner is an essential requirement for all personnel who must communicate with patients, their families and other staff members.*
Application:	*This policy shall apply to all members of the medical staff, employees, volunteers and employees of outsider contractors, all of whom shall be referred to for the purposes of this policy as "staff".*
Cross-References:	P1.6; P2.2.1; P1.3.3; P1.6
Policies:	1. Staff shall treat and speak with all patients, their families and friends with courtesy, respect, dignity and modesty, showing concern but at the same time acting with professional reserve. 2. Every oral communication with a patient, a patient's representative, a patient's family or a visitor or another staff member has just as much importance to the health and legal rights of the patient as if it were in writing. 3. Staff shall always introduce themselves to the patient, the patient's family and the patient's representative. 4. Patients shall be asked how they wish to be addressed. They shall not initially be asked whether they mind being addressed by the first name. Adult patients shall initially be addressed by their last name, unless the patient asks to be addressed by their first names. Addressing older patients by their first names may be regarded as demeaning and patronizing, even if patients do not appear to object. 5. For patients' names that may be difficult to pronounce or may not be pronounced according to

English usage (or French in a French-speaking institution), the patient, family or friends shall be asked for the correct pronunciation, which shall be recorded on the front page of the patient's record in a phonetic manner.

6.   At no time shall a patient's condition, physical appearance, clothing, name, or religious, political, racial, national or ethnic origin, accent or dialect, sexual conduct, sexual orientation, personal life or personality be discussed either positively or negatively by any member of staff except in so far as the provision of healthcare requires such discussion, nor shall any assumptions be made as a result of such matters without evidence supporting such conclusions.

7.   Any staff member who speaks English or in the case of a French hospital, French, or speaks with an accent that may not be understood by the patient or by the patient's family or representative, shall advise the patient or the family or representative that if they do not understand, that they should feel free to ask for clarification.

8.   Staff shall not joke nor make light of the patient's condition since the patient may consider it to be a serious or a sensitive matter.

9.   Staff shall not initiate or respond to any discussion of religious, cultural, social, ethical or political issues.

10.   Staff shall not comment to patients, their families or their friends or visitors on any matter regarding the policies of the institution, or on the relations between the institution and other parties, or on any matter regarding the relations between staff members or between staff members and the institution.

11.   No staff member shall use crude or socially unacceptable language or gestures in front of patients, their family or friends or visitors.

12.   Staff shall not use slang or off-colour language in describing any part of the anatomy. Even if a patient uses inappropriate language, health personnel should not. This particularly applies to any reference which could be taken, even remotely, to have sexual connotations.

13. In conversing with a patient or family, staff shall avoid the use of hand gestures which may be understood differently from what is intended.

14. Staff shall make every effort to determine whether the patient has any cultural, religious or social attitudes that may affect his or her ability to respond to or participate in diagnosis, care or treatment. Such findings will be recorded in the patient's record. While assistance from the family, friends or the representatives may be obtained, care shall be taken to ensure that the attitudes are those of the patient and not those of others who may assume that those are the patient's attitudes.

15. In advising the patient or representative, staff shall be very specific in use of language that the patient or representative can understand given their current mental state, their familiarity with the current condition, and their educational and cultural understanding. Any explanation shall be of sufficient length and content to enable the particular patient to understand and to take whatever action may be necessary, but should not be so long or complex that information that is not required makes it difficult for the patient to understand.

16. When a foreign language translator or a sign language translator is required, a translator shall be obtained through the patient services' office of the institution. Translators brought by the patient or family are not to be used unless the patient services' office is able to recognize their competency to translate.

17. If the patient is present during a staff conversation with the family and friends, and is aware of the conversation, staff shall speak directly to the patient while including others who are present. Care should be taken not to give the impression that the patient is being excluded from the discussion, such as by referring to the patient in the third person.

18. Staff shall make certain that the patient is mentally capable of understanding the discussion and is capable of expressing questions, instructions and seeking assistance, and that a family member or friend is not imposing their will on the patient or exercising undue pressure, or making statements that do not reflect those

	that would be made by the patient.
	19. If the patient disagrees with the caregiver, every effort should be made to accommodate the patient's wishes as long as the patient is fully informed of the consequences, except in those situations in which to do so would not meet professional standards of care or ethical standards, or if such an action is forbidden by hospital policy or by law. In these situations, the patient must be informed of this and offered a second opinion. In no case shall a procedure be imposed on a patient, as long as the patient is mentally capable of consenting or refusing.

Policy 3.2: Patient Relations — Expectations of Patients	
Objective:	*The purpose of this policy is to convey to patients and their families that the provision of health services is a partnership of the institution and its staff, and the patient with the patient's family. To make this partnership work, the healthcare provider, consisting of both the institution and the staff, provides diagnosis, treatment and care at a reasonable standard within the resources available to it. The patient and the patient's family must also meet certain expectations in response to the provider's efforts.*
Application:	*All medical staff, employees, patients and their families.*
Cross-References:	F5; F6
Policies:	1. The patient shall advise the provider of: a. all information requested regarding the patient's health in as complete and truthful a manner as possible; b. the identity of all prescription and non-prescription drugs or medications being taken, including the name, dosage and frequency taken; c. any changes in the drugs or medications being taken including their discontinuance, dosage, frequency and any changes in their designation including change in the brand name, or changes to or from a brand product to a generic product; d. any reactions to any medications, medical, or health-related procedures, either currently or in the past; e. any reactions to any matter with which the patient has been in contact either currently or in the past, including food or drink, physical substances contacted, odours or changes in atmospheric conditions; f. any medical condition from which the patient is currently suffering or has had in the past, and any medical, surgical or health-related procedures in the past; g. any medical condition from which a relative

		has suffered, causing death, or is currently suffering;
	h.	any activity in which the patient has been or is currently engaged about which the provider inquires, including any changes in such activities, including the use of alcohol or recreational drugs, physical activity or sports; and
	i.	any contemplated or completed travel to any tropical or subtropical location, or any location in which health or sanitary conditions may be limited or in which the standards of practice may be different from what the patient habitually encounters.
	2.	The patient shall attend all appointments, and shall reschedule any appointments which cannot be kept within two days prior to the appointment date.
	3.	The patient shall attend all diagnostic, and treatment referrals as recommended.
	4.	The patient shall advise the institution of the names and contacts of all other providers from whom health services are being received including non-medical providers such as dentists, chiropractors, optometrists, and mental health therapists.
	5.	The patient shall endeavour to patronize one pharmacy only, in order to maintain consistency and oversight of all of the patient's pharmacy needs.

Policy 3.3: Patient Relations — Physical Contact between Staff and Patients	
Objective:	*The public has become extremely aware and sensitive to the possibility of sexual harassment, assault and generally inappropriate behaviour of a sexual or potentially sexual nature. This awareness has been applied specifically to health services, educational institutions and religious institutions. These suspicions have translated into actual and potential lawsuits brought by patients who either were subject to behaviour that was inappropriate, or they thought that they were. In either case, even the threat of a lawsuit can have a devastating effect on professional careers, and on the reputation of a health institution or other provider, even if the matter is discontinued. For this reason, this policy deals not only with actual physical contact but also with situations in which the opportunity to have inappropriate physical contact may exist, even if such contact does not occur.*
Application:	*This policy applies to all employees, members of the medical staff and volunteers who may be involved directly or indirectly with any aspect of patient care. For the purposes of this section, all such individuals will be referred to as "staff".*
Cross-References:	
Policies:	1. No staff shall touch a patient unless it is absolutely necessary for the examination, diagnosis or treatment. It is noted that in some cultures the touching of another individual, even a child, may have extremely negative connotations. Even in North American society and even where a patient appears to be relaxed and friendly, touching for any reason other than for the provision of care, may be resented, or may be misinterpreted.
	2. Prior to touching a patient, the patient shall be advised that touching is necessary along with the reasons for the physical contact, and the nature of the physical contact intended.
	3. No patient shall be left unclothed either wholly or partially in view of any other person other than the person who is caring for the patient, except where this is required for the purpose of care, diagnosis or treatment.

4. When a staff member examines a patient of the opposite sex, a staff member of the same sex as the patient shall be present, or at least a door to where staff of the same sex is present should be slightly ajar.

5. Every consulting or examining room shall be furnished in such a way so that if a patient attempts to make physical advances on a staff member, there must always be an easy way to escape from the room. A panic button shall be placed in all consulting and examining rooms.

6. Any advances by a patient or anyone else that have a sexual innuendo or may be interpreted as such, shall be politely and firmly rejected. The staff member shall leave the room, report the incident to the supervisor or other administrative authority who shall investigate the matter and take whatever action is appropriate, and shall record the incident immediately.

7. At no time shall health personnel make any show of intimacy either by word, gesture or physical contact, which could be taken as a sexual advance.

8. Sexual intimacy of any sort between personnel and patients, their relatives or friends is strictly forbidden, as long as the patient relationship exists.

Policy 3.4: Patient Relations — Terminating the Patient Relationship	
Objective:	*The importance of this policy is to minimize the risk of a lawsuit brought by the patient or client alleging that the provider has abandoned the patient or client and as a result has caused injury. This risk is present with physicians, dentists and particularly therapists including mental health therapists upon whom the patient or client relies over an extended period of time.*
Application:	*This policy applies to all board members, members of medical staff committees and members of any other committee operating under the authority of the institution, all employees and volunteers.*
Cross-References:	F6; F11; F45
Policies:	1. There are situations in which the patient-provider relationship is such that the healthcare provider is not able to serve the patient in a manner that is likely to be productive, or according to accepted professional standards. Such a situation may arise under a number of circumstances, including the following in which the patient:
	a. refuses to follow the advice of the provider or to follow a treatment plan as agreed without consulting the provider, *i.e.*, non-compliance;
	b. repeatedly misses appointments;
	c. is unco-operative with the provider such as by refusing to divulge information required for the continuation of advice, treatment or care, or by misleading the provider regarding symptoms or other matters which may affect the advice, treatment or care; and
	d. is physically aggressive or threatening towards the provider or other staff or patients, is verbally abusive, or whose conduct is otherwise disruptive in the facility, though a certain tolerance may be allowed in situations in which the patient is suffering from a disorder which gives rise to conduct of this type.
	2. When situations arise in which a productive relationship with the patient is no longer possible, the

	provider is entitled to terminate the relationship. The advice of the risk manager must be obtained before this step is taken.
	3. In ending the relationship, it is important that the following procedure be followed and that careful documentation be made as evidence that the steps were in fact followed. This is to lessen the risk of a patient allegation of abandonment, that is that the provider has terminated the relationship upon which the patient was depending and as a result, the patient has suffered injury.
	4. When such a situation arises, an oral warning shall be given to the patient that the patient's conduct makes it difficult or even impossible to treat or provide service, and that if it continues the relationship will have to be terminated.
	5. If the patient's conduct continues, a formal meeting shall take place with the provider during which a record is made. The patient shall be advised as to the problem, the consequences of the conduct and the difficulty of the provider in providing service. If the problem occurs in an institution, the social worker, or risk manager shall also be present. The patient shall be clearly advised that if the conduct continues, the relationship will be terminated and that the patient will have to seek services elsewhere. A time of possible termination shall be set.
	6. The patient should also be told at the meeting that if the relationship is terminated, every reasonable effort will be made to refer the patient to another provider, but that no guarantee can be made that the other provider will accept the patient. A registered mail letter from the formal meeting outlining what was discussed shall be sent to the patient.
	7. If the patient's conduct is not altered within the time period set, a registered letter shall be sent to the patient terminating the relationship for the reasons outlined in the previous letter. The patient shall be advised that if another provider is desired a call should be made to the terminating provider of care, and that an attempt will be made to suggest alternates though it will then be the patient's responsibility to make the necessary arrangements.

8. The letter shall also advise that copies of the patient's file will be made available to the new provider at the instructions of the patient, for a minimal charge. A request for a release of the file should be included asking that it be signed and returned.

9. It is important that the patient be given at least two weeks to find a new provider. The patient shall be informed of this, and that after a specified date, a note will be placed in the file so that further appointments will not be made, and any written requests for care or opinions be responded to advising that since the individual is no longer a patient the request will have to be forwarded to the new provider. If no forwarding address has been supplied, a request should be made for one.

10. Any contact made by the patient with the provider by mail, telephone, electronically or in person shall be reported immediately to the risk manager.

Policy 3.5: Patient Relations — Consultations and Referrals	
Objective:	*This policy is designed to establish a procedure for referrals outside the location or facility where the patient is currently being treated. It therefore applies not only to consultations from a family physician, for example, to a specialist, but from one specialist to another, from a non-physician health professional to a physician or vice versa, or referrals outside for diagnostic tests. It refers to anything in which the patient, or information about a patient, such as a blood or urine sample, leaves the facility for analysis elsewhere.*
	The purpose ordinarily is to obtain further information or opinion to enable the initial provider to treat or diagnose, or to continue the treatment in a more specialized way beyond that which can be given by the initial provider.
	This practice carries with it an inherent risk of error which may result in the incorrect treatment of the patient, the failure to treat or diagnose, or a delay in the treatment or diagnosis, all of which can result in injury or alleged injury, and thus has the potential of liability or other legal ramifications.
	Invariably, the risk arises out of a communication problem. The information conveyed or the information or opinion returning to the originating provider was incorrect, did not correctly respond to the request originally made, did not arrive or was not seen, was misinterpreted, or was delayed. Most of these problems do not involve professional judgement. They are purely administrative or even clerical matters, which can be limited through policies and procedures, as long as those involved understand the importance of following the policies and procedures, and follow them precisely.
	Problems also arise because of the manner in which the communication took place. The specialist receiving the request for an opinion for example, may not have been given sufficient background information, or the reason for the referral, and therefore has based an opinion or treatment on information which is incomplete. The response may not in fact, directly respond to the needs of the health professional who requested the referral or the opinion. In other words, there has not been a meeting of minds. The advice which is given may not have included

sufficient information on the course of action to be taken, which can also cause difficulties. Both parties involved may be assuming that the other knows certain matters, which in fact is not true.

A further complication deals with the communications failure between the referring health provider and the patient. The patient may not understand the importance of following up on the referral. The patient may be confused as to who makes the appointment, or the importance of keeping the appointment. It can be alleged by the patient in any legal action that if he had known that it was that important to see the specialist, he would have done so, but was under the impression that while it was advisable, he did not appreciate that he could suffer injury by not going. Whether this is true or not is not relevant. It still is a risk of liability which should be minimized.

A final risk arising from consultations and referrals is the failure of the originating health provider to follow up. If a report or response is not received within the expected time period either from the specialist to whom the patient was referred or from a diagnostic service, the allegation can be made that it was negligence not to be aware of this and to follow up. Similarly, if the information received in response did not match the request or is obviously incorrect, it may be considered negligence not to do a further follow-up.

The purpose, therefore, of this policy and any form is to provide accuracy and completeness in communications between healthcare providers of either the same or differing discipline in a timely manner, and between the health professional and the patient. The purpose of a form is to assist in the carrying out of the procedure so that nothing is forgotten, and that there is a record that the procedure was carried out. In the event of legal proceedings, this will provide evidence in the defence of any allegations

The approach in the policy is two-pronged. The first type of approach concentrates on the communication itself from the initiating healthcare provider such as a request for certain diagnostic tests or a letter seeking the opinion of a specialist or from a healthcare provider of a different discipline. The second type of approach is to have a procedure to ensure and record that this was accomplished.

Application:	*This applies to any health professional or other person attending to the needs of a patient who requires outside services or a consultation. It may apply to a private family physician who wishes to refer a patient to a specialist, or to a specialist non-physician professional such as a physiotherapist, a psychologist or a nutritionist. It may equally apply to a dentist who refers the patient to a physician either for advice or treatment, or to an orthodontist. Similarly, it could apply to a social worker or psychologist who refers a patient to a medical specialist. It may apply to a private practitioner's office, or to a larger establishment with numerous health professionals on staff such as a clinic, or to an in-patient or out-patient institution, or to a referring professional in a non-health facility such as a school or a prison.*
Cross-References:	F5; F26; F27; F28; F29
Policies:	1. **Request for external consultation or referral.** All requests for an external opinion, diagnosis, or treatment whether by form or by letter shall include the following information. Each item is to be numbered so that the response can relate directly to specific items. a. name of patient (family name first); b. identification number; c. address and (daytime) telephone number; d. sex; e. birth date; f. weight, height; g. name of person acting on behalf of the patient (if applicable); h. referring physician or other health provider; i. address and (daytime) telephone number; j. date of request; k. healthcare provider referred to; l. address and (daytime) telephone number; m. who made or is to make appointment;

n.   date and time of appointment;

o.   purpose of referral;

p.   medical history; and

q.   specific issues to be addressed.

2.   **Tracking**

a.   A system shall be established to make certain that requests for external diagnosis, care or treatment, or an opinion are responded to in an accurate and timely fashion so that errors in the communication of the request and the response will be kept to a minimum.

b.   A procedure shall be established that will accomplish the following:

   i.   notification to the person requesting the external consultation or referral if the response has not been received by a particular date;

   ii.   the failure to receive a response should trigger a further request or such other action in order to obtain a response, including contact with the patient;

   iii. the failure in a response to respond accurately to the request shall also trigger a further request for clarification;

   iv.   on receipt of a response in an office or institution, there shall be a procedure whereby the response will immediately be forwarded to the provider who requested it along with the patient's file, for assessment and necessary action; and

   v   a record shall be kept that the procedure has been followed and a record of whatever action has been taken.

Policy 3.6: Patient Relations — Telephone and Other Electronic Orders	
Objective:	*Because of the risk of errors in oral communication, it is necessary that all personnel take exceptional precautions to ensure that what they say and what they hear convey the same information, and are absolutely accurate. The accuracy of orders protects patients' safety. This policy is also directed towards limiting the use of such orders in order not only to limit the inherent risks of patient injury due to inaccuracies in the orders, but also to provide for defence material in case of a lawsuit against a healthcare provider.*
Application:	*All members of the medical staff, and all employees involved in both the giving and receiving of treatment or diagnostic instructions.*
Cross-References:	
Policies:	1. Orders by telephone or other electronic means shall only be given and received when it is not possible or practical for the person giving the order to be physically present, or if there is no other individual present who has the authority to give such an order, or if it is not possible or practical to issue the order in a written format and to have it placed in the patient's record.
	2. Any person giving an order by telephone or other electronic means shall identify themselves by name and position, and provide such information regarding their location so that contact may be made with them if necessary.
	3. Any person receiving a telephone order shall record the order in writing and read it back to the person giving the order to confirm its correctness, along with the identity, position and contact information of the person giving the order, along with the date and time when the order is received.
	4. No conversation over the telephone regarding a patient shall take place under any circumstances in which either party may be overheard by anyone other than other staff members.
	5. No order in any electronic format including fax or by computer shall be visible to any person other than staff members.

Policy 4.1:	Consent to Treatment — Obtaining Patient's Consent
Objective:	*This policy recognizes that the basic and most important principle upon which **all** treatment, diagnosis and care is given is that the patient, or someone who is legally authorized to act for the patient, has consented to such treatment, diagnosis and care. The only exceptions are specifically authorized by law, such as an emergency in which neither the patient nor anyone on the patient's behalf is able to consent, and a delay until consent or substitute consent would be detrimental to the patient's health. Exceptions are also recognized in certain cases of mental illness and communicable diseases prescribed by legislation. It also recognizes that the right of the patient is not only a right to consent, but equally a right to refuse treatment, regardless of the consequences. The patient has a right to refuse diagnosis, care and treatment even if professional opinion recommends it. These principles establish this right on the understanding that any medical, surgical, diagnostic, treatment or care given to or proposed for a patient is an interference with the patient's body over which the patient, except in those legally recognized exceptions, has absolute authority.* *It is often thought that consent only applies to surgery. In fact, it applies to any interference with the patient's body, including prescribed drugs. Regardless of the medical necessity or desirability, the primary right of a patient is the legal right to prevent any other person from interfering with his or her body, unless the law specifically allows for an exception to this right. Every form of diagnosis, treatment and care depends on this right being relinquished through the consent process. Only then is the legal relationship between the patient and the caregiver or health institution formed. Once that occurs, various other rights and obligations arise, such as the right to a reasonable standard of care.* *For a more complete discussion of Canadian law relating to consent, see "The Canadian Law of Consent to Treatment", 3rd ed. by Lorne E. Rozovsky (Markham, ON: LexisNexis Butterworths, 2003) endorsed by the Canadian Health Information Management Association.*
Application:	*This policy applies to every person who is to receive diagnostic or treatment services. It applies to all such persons regardless of their mental capacity and regard-*

	less of whether or not such a person is in police custody or other custody authorized by law. The policy applies whether or not the person is an adult or child, whether married or single, and regardless of citizenship, and regardless of whether the person is insured.
Cross-References:	P4.6; P4.7; F1; F2; F7; F11; F14; F15; F16; F17; F18; F19; F20; F21; F22; F24; F25
Policies:	1. No diagnosis, care, treatment, medication or any examination or routine procedure shall take place without the consent of the patient, or if the patient is not able to consent either because of mental or physical incapacity, or because of legislation which removes the authority of the patient to consent.
	2. Professional opinion that the patient requires care cannot overrule the right of a patient to decide whether or not to have care.
	3. Professional ethics or religious beliefs of a health professional shall not overrule the right of a patient to make this decision.
	4. The consent to care or treatment consists of an agreement to undergo such care or treatment, and does not consist of signing a consent form which is required simply as evidence that the patient or someone on the patient's behalf has consented, and may in some instances be required by legislation.
	5. No consent may be accepted if the person giving the consent has not been given sufficient information to make such a decision, and is mentally capable of understanding the information given as the basis of the decision and the implications of consenting.
	6. No staff member shall impose treatment, diagnosis or care on a patient against the will or refusal of the patient, for any reason including the ethics or religious beliefs of the staff member.
	7. Consent is a process by which the patient or someone legally authorized to act on behalf of the patient, is given sufficient information on which a decision is made regarding whether or not to undergo treatment.
	8. Consent to undergo a procedure or the refusal to

undergo a procedure may be expressed in writing, verbally or through signs or gestures.

9. The process of informing the patient, assessing the patient's ability to consent, and obtaining the patient's consent shall be documented in the prescribed form for those procedures designated from time to time, and in any case shall be documented in the patient's record.

10. For procedures for which there is no consent form, the person carrying out the consent process shall document the process on the patient's record.

11. A patient may withdraw consent at any time, including during a procedure, assuming that the patient is mentally capable of receiving sufficient information and advice, and assessing this information and advice and making this decision.

12. The requirement that the patient be given sufficient information to make an informed consent to undergo a procedure applies equally to making a decision not to undergo a procedure.

13. No involuntary treatment shall be given for mental illness or any communicable disease unless the provisions of legislation authorize such treatment.

14. In an emergency situation in which any delay in treatment may jeopardize the life or health of the patient, treatment shall only proceed if the patient or someone authorized to act on behalf of the patient consents, or if neither the patient nor any other authorized person is capable of giving a valid consent.

Policy 4.2: Consent to Treatment — Telephone Consents	
Objective:	*Ordinarily, consent to treatment or any other procedure is given by the patient in the presence of the care providers who are able to provide the information upon which the consent decision is based. However, it is recognized that there are situations in which the patient is not either legally or mentally capable of receiving or considering the information and making such a decision. In such cases, someone else must act on behalf of the patient and do what the patient would ordinarily do. The preference is that such a substitute should be physically present with the caregiver when going through the consent process.*
	However, there are situations in which this is not possible, and contact with the substitute can only be made by telephone. This raises a number of legal risks. The first is to make certain that the substitute is in fact authorized to consent on the patient's behalf, and that there is written documentation which provides evidence of the consent even though the substitute is not in a position to be able to sign any documentation.
	Nevertheless, a telephone consent may be the only practical alternative. In taking such consent, a number of guidelines must be followed in order to minimize the liability risks of not having a consent that can later be proven to be valid.
Application:	*This policy applies to all situations requiring consent in which the patient for mental, physical or legal reasons cannot take part in the consent process, and that the consent of a substitute can only be obtained by telephone.*
Cross-References:	F18
Policies:	1. Consent to a procedure by telephone shall only take place when a patient is either mentally or legally incapable of consenting, and an appropriate substitute is not personally available within an acceptable time period prior to the administration of the procedure.
	2. When a telephone consent is required, it shall be made by the attending physician who shall provide full identity and contact information to the telephone contact.
	3. Queries shall be made to ensure that an appropriate substitute has been reached, including information

on the relationship of the contact to the patient, and that the contact is willing to make a decision regarding the procedure.

4. A second person shall listen in on the call, and the contact shall be advised that this is the case for the purpose of providing evidence that the call has taken place.

5. The contact shall be advised as to the name and identity of the witness listening in on the call.

6. The caller shall advise the contact of all information that would ordinarily be provided to the patient or a substitute who is physically present, so that a valid informed consent can be made.

7. The contact shall be asked for all pertinent information that would ordinarily be requested of the patient, including past medical history, current medications, and allergies, and any further information that might influence the provision of treatment and care.

8. The telephone contact shall be given the opportunity to ask questions.

9. The contact shall be asked to provide the name and contact information of the patient's regular physician and reasonable steps shall be taken to contact the physician and obtain verification of any information given by the telephone contact.

10. A record shall be kept in the appropriate form of the information given and received during the telephone call, the names and contact information of the contact, and of the details of the consent process.

11. The contact shall be given all sufficient information to be able to further contact the caller and any other person involved in the care of the patient.

12. A record shall be maintained that this policy has been followed, or that it has not been followed and the reasons for it not being followed.

13. The substitute shall be encouraged to attend the patient personally.

Policy 4.3: Consent to Treatment — Refusal of Treatment	
Objective:	*The purpose of this policy is to protect the patient's legal right to refuse care or treatment, even that care or treatment which may be beneficial, and to protect the patient's right to be advised to the greatest extent possible so that the decision to refuse care or treatment is based on as complete information and advice as is possible under the circumstances. By protecting the patient's rights in this regard, this policy aims to reduce the risk of liability exposure of the healthcare provider and the institution for contravening what is a basic legal right of the patient.*
Application:	*This policy applies particularly to members of the medical staff and to employees who are directly involved in providing care and treatment to patients and in requesting those patients for their consent to administer such care and or treatment.*
Cross-References:	F17; F22
Policies:	1. This institution recognizes the absolute right of every individual to refuse care, treatment or medication, even in those situations in which professional staff are of the opinion that the patient requires these services.
	2. It is recognized that a patient may only be treated against his or her wishes if circumstances exist whereby a mental illness is in evidence. In such a circumstance treatment can only be given if those circumstances exactly fit the provisions as outlined in the relevant provincial *Mental Health Act*, and the procedure of the Act must be followed precisely. If these two factors are not met, any treatment or care imposed against the voluntary consent of the patient, may be considered as assault and battery. Similarly, treatment for a communicable disease also cannot be treated against the will of the patient unless the provisions of the communicable diseases legislation are met precisely.
	3. As required by the consent process (see Policy 4.1), the patient is to be informed of the nature, risks and benefits of the procedure, the risks of not undergoing the procedure, and any reasonable alternatives with the nature, risks and benefits of those alternatives.

4. If the patient refuses care prior to being informed, the patient is to be advised that the refusal cannot be accepted until the information has been given.

5. Neither the professional judgment nor the ethics of any staff member shall overrule the decision of the patient.

6. If a patient is mentally capable of making a decision regarding care or treatment and refuses such care or treatment and is a danger to himself or herself, or to others in the institution or the property of the institution, a decision may be made to temporarily restrain the patient or provide emergency care solely for the purpose of restraint. If necessary, staff shall summon the assistance of security or the police.

7. If a patient is not mentally capable of making a decision regarding care or treatment, and such refusal will or is likely to cause imminent injury or death, a decision regarding care or treatment shall be sought from the patient's substitute decision-maker. If no substitute is available, the necessary care or treatment shall be given without consent as an emergency.

8. In the middle of a procedure, a patient may rescind any consent previously given, though the patient shall be advised of the potential consequences of such withdrawal.

9. Any action taken under this policy shall be recorded along with all facts leading up to such action.

Policy 4.4: Consent to Treatment — Consent of Minors	
Objective:	*The purpose of the policy is to clarify and to remove any misunderstandings of staff regarding the legal rights of children with respect to consenting to their own health care. The policy is designed to protect the legal rights of children, and at the same time control the risk of liability of staff and the institution if such rights are not respected. The purpose of the policy is also designed to clarify those situations in which a child may not have the legal right to consent or to refuse his or her own care or treatment. However, this policy must be reviewed by legal counsel in order to conform with provincial legislation relating to minors giving consent for their own medical care. Several provinces have specific legislative provisions dealing with the age of consent, including New Brunswick, British Columbia and Quebec.*
Application:	*This policy applies to all members of the medical staff, and all other staff members who are directly involved in the diagnosis, care or treatment of minor patients, and who are involved in advising those patients or their parents or guardians to obtain consent.*
Cross-References:	F20; F21; F23
Policies:	1. Except where provincial legislation specifically states otherwise (*include provincial legislation on age of consent*), any person regardless of age may consent to or reject care or treatment if he or she is mentally capable of understanding the information given upon which a consent decision is to be made, and mentally capable of understanding what it is to make such a decision.
	2. Any minor who is regarded as being able to make a consent decision, shall be treated as an adult and no adult shall be asked to participate in the decision-making process without the agreement of the patient.
	3. Special care shall be taken to insure that any child who is able to consent on his or her own behalf, is not pressured or overtly influenced by adults or other children.
	4. If a child is not able to consent, the decision shall be

sought from one or both parents, a person standing in the place of a parent, or any adult sibling.

5. If a child is not able to consent and a parent or other substitute refuses to consent, the risk manager shall be notified and legal counsel consulted to obtain a court-authorized consent.

6. In the case of a child who is unable to consent, and it is unclear as to which parent has the legal authority to consent on behalf of the child, the matter shall immediately referred to the risk manager and legal counsel.

7. In the case of a child who is unable to consent, and the parents or guardians disagree on a matter of consent, the case shall be referred to the risk manager and legal counsel. Unless there is legal authorization to the contrary or in circumstances which would invalidate the decision of one of the parents, the decision of the parent who has custody of the child will ordinarily be accepted.

8. Any situation in which a third party is or appears to be interfering or attempting to influence any person making a treatment decision for a child shall be reported to the risk manager who shall advise legal counsel.

Policy 4.5: Consent to Treatment — Emergency Consent	
Objective:	*The purpose of this policy is to assist healthcare professionals in obtaining consent or to deal with situations in which consent is not mentally or physically possible, and an emergency exists requiring immediate treatment. This policy only applies when what is designated as a medico-legal emergency exists. This is defined within the policy, and may not be always be the same as an emergency in strictly medical terms.* *The importance of the medico-legal emergency is that it is an exception to the rule that individuals cannot be treated without their consent or the consent of someone who is authorized to give consent on their behalf, unless legislation specifically allows for such treatment to take place. For this exception to apply, it is necessary that the circumstances fit the definition precisely. In some provinces or territories, where legislation exists, the circumstances must fit exactly within the words of the definition.*
Application:	*This policy applies to all staff who are faced with obtaining the consent of a patient prior to treatment, and who must make the decision as to whether a medico-legal emergency exists so that treatment can proceed without consent.*
Cross-References:	P4.1; F19
Policies:	1. If a patient is mentally capable of understanding the information and advice given for the purpose of making a decision as to whether or not to undergo recommended care or treatment, the consent of the patient shall be required even in cases of emergencies. 2. For the purpose of this policy an emergency is defined as a situation in which a delay in the care or treatment of a patient is likely to result in injury or death. 3. If an emergency as defined by this policy exists, and the patient is not mentally capable of understanding and therefore not capable of making a decision whether to consent or not, consent shall be sought from an appropriate substitute, such as a spouse, a child who is mentally capable, or a sibling.

| | 4. | In cases of emergency, a precise record shall be made of those factors supporting the determination that an emergency exists and as to the patient's ability or inability to consent. |

Policy 4.6: Consent to Treatment — Language Consents and Comprehension	
Objective:	*While the official or working language of the institution may be English, French or bilingual, the institution cannot ignore the necessity of communicating with patients in their own languages other than English or French. This not only ensures accurate communication between caregivers and patients, thus helping to maintain required standards of care and avoiding miscommunication and patient injury, but also plays a vital role in matters of consent. Because consent or refusal to consent is based on information and advice communicated to the patient, this cannot be done except in a language that is understood by the patient, or by the person who is acting as a substitute consent giver. In addition, staffs are encouraged to learn as much as possible about the cultural and religious attitudes of patients from other religious, ethnic and cultural backgrounds towards health-care, in order to provide a better understanding for communication generally and for communication in seeking consent in particular.*
Application:	*This policy applies to all members of the medical staff and any other professional having direct contact with patients and their families, especially those of other ethnic, cultural or religious groups.*
Cross-References:	P4.1; F13
Policies:	1. As part of the assessment of every patient following admission, a determination will be made as to the ability of the patient to understand spoken English (or French).
	2. Linguistic comprehension shall be determined by means of a two-way conversation related to their medical condition and by asking the patient to orally provide information in terms more extensive than a positive or negative response to questions.
	3. Linguistic comprehension shall not be determined simply by asking the patient or a family member or other person whether or not the patient speaks or understands English (or French).
	4. No patient shall be asked to sign any consent or other document in a language which the patient does

not understand.

5. In assessing a patient who does speak or understand English (or French), a determination shall be made as to whether a patient has the comprehension ability to understand information, advice or questions presented to the patient in the manner in which such information, advice or questions are presented.

6. If it is determined that a patient cannot understand, for whatever reason, what is said to them, any response given by the patient shall not be acted on. Efforts shall be made to present the information in a manner in which the patient can understand.

7. If a patient's inability to understand or communicate is compromised by linguistic inability or deafness, a translator or sign language specialist certified by the institution shall be used.

Policy 4.7: Consent to Treatment — Consent to Experimental or Research Procedures	
Objective:	*This policy is designed to ensure that members of the medical staff and other staff members involved in experimental or research procedures are fully aware of the very strict consent requirements ordinarily imposed by law and, in addition, to the requirements imposed by the Tri-Council Policy Statement. Following these requirements will assist in the management of liability risks as well as the potential loss of funding and accreditation which could jeopardize research programs in the institution.*
Application:	*This policy applies not only to members of the medical staff directly involved in experimental or research procedures, but all those having administrative responsibilities involving such matters, along with the medical director and members of the Institutional Review Board of the institution.*
Cross-References:	P4.1
Policies:	1. No research procedure funded under the Canadian Institutes of Health Research, the Social Sciences and Humanities Research Council of Canada or the Natural Sciences and Engineering Research Council shall take place without its approval by the Ethics Research Board.
	2. No procedure funded as noted shall take place in or with the involvement of the institution unless the requirements of the Tri-Council Policy Statement are strictly followed.
	3. No member of the staff shall conduct or be involved in any research procedure under this policy with specific approval of the Ethics Research Board and the Board of Trustees.
	4. All staff involved in research under this policy shall be informed in writing of the provisions of the Tri-Council Policy Statement and any further requirements that may be added from time to time, and shall be required to agree in writing to abide by the required provisions.
	5. Legal counsel, the risk manager and the medical advisory committee shall review the implementation of

the Tri-Council Policy Statement on a semi-annual basis, and at such other times that developments require such review, and may add further requirements to it.

6. The Board of Trustees having received the advice of legal counsel, the risk manager and the medical advisory committee shall determine whether any or all of the Tri-Council Policy Statement shall apply to any research or experimental procedures that are not funded by any of the three councils, but may be funded through other sources, and whether any additional requirements shall be imposed.

7. The medical director shall have the responsibility of monitoring compliance with the Tri-Council Policy Statement and any other policies that may be adopted within the institution, and shall report any infractions to the credentials committee.

8. The risk manager shall be responsible to ensure that the requirements for the valid consent of patients to all research and experimental procedures regardless of any external funding shall be followed, and in finding any irregulairities shall report them to the executive director and the medical director.

Policy 5.1: Record Keeping, Handling and Maintenance — Recording Information	
Objective:	*Despite the move from written records to the collecting, recording and storing of health information by electronic means, written recording continues to be widely used within the health system and will undoubtedly continue to play a major role. Regardless of the means of collection and recording, errors in the recording of information continue to result in injury to patients, and as a result provide a risk of liability for health facilities and health staff. The use of predesigned forms and the set format of computerized records may reduce this risk, since both establish a format requiring the person recording information to record it according to certain predetermined standards. However, it does not remove the risk, just as handwritten recording also does not remove the risk.*
	The fundamental principle in documenting health information is that the recording of information is intended to be a communication to others who may read it, including a reminder to the person who recorded it. Unless the information is recorded with this in mind, errors may occur, individuals will act on the information recorded and errors of information or the failure to record information may result in someone either taking improper action with respect to the patient, or failing to take appropriate action, either of which may result in patient injury, and a subsequent lawsuit on the basis of negligence.
	For a more complete explanation see "Canadian Health Information: A Practical Legal and Risk Management Guide", 3rd ed. by Lorne E. Rozovsky and Noela J. Inions (Markham, ON: Butterworths Canada, 2002), c. 12, "Documenting Health Information".
Application:	*All staff members who record and use recorded health information, and health information management personnel.*
Cross-References:	F3; F5; F6; F7; F27; F28; F29; F30; F31; F35
Policies:	1. All information recorded about any patient is to be recorded with absolute accuracy.
	2. Information received from outside the institution that is to be added to the records of the institution shall include identification as to the source and the

date on which it was received, and any efforts that have been made to confirm its authenticity.

3. Entries to any record shall conform to the standards of terminology prescribed for use in this institution.

4. Abbreviations used in entries shall conform to the prescribed list of abbreviations established for use in the institution.

5. Information received from an external source containing terminology or abbreviations that do not conform to the prescribed list of this institution shall include an explanatory note listing the equivalent terms of abbreviations.

6. All entries made on paper shall be in pen.

7. All entries shall be written in block print, or in cursive that is absolutely legible to any person who is not familiar with the recorder's handwriting.

8. Record concisely. Only essential information is to be included. Information is not to be repeated within the same entry.

9. Record events chronologically.

10. Dates are to be recorded in the following manner: month (using the letter abbreviation), day, year.

11. All times are to be recorded according to the 24-hour clock.

12. All measurements are to be recorded according to the metric system. Information received in the Imperial system are to be recorded as received with the equivalent according to the metric system immediately after in brackets.

13. Recording of all information shall take place immediately on receipt or as quickly as is practical. Records shall not be grouped for completion of a number at once.

14. Do not rush when making entries.

15. The person who was directly involved in the event being recorded shall be the person who records the information.

16. All entries shall be signed, or initialled, along with the assigned number given to staff in the institution for the purpose of identifying persons making entries into the record.

17. All stations shall have an up-to-date list of persons authorized to make record entries. As new lists are published old lists are to be immediately destroyed.

18. A uniform system of handwriting numerals and certain letters shall be established, and shall be followed throughout the facility.

19. Handwritten errors in the records shall be corrected openly and honestly, noting that an error has occurred, and noting the correction which shall be signed and dated.

20. Staff shall not make editorial comments in the patient records relating to the performance of other staff members or other institutions or healthcare providers, institutional or government policies, or any person unless such comments are clearly necessary for the effective recording of information for the purposes of caring for the patient.

21. Following the making of an entry into the records regardless of whether the record is paper or electronic, the entry shall be read and checked for accuracy and compliance with this policy.

22. Precise notes of the information and advice given shall be entered into the patient's record, including any questions or comments by the patient or the patient's representative. The note shall include the date and time, and the names of those who were present at the discussion.

23. The entry into the record shall be made by the person leading the discussion with the patient, and not someone else who is taking notes.

24. The information and advice as recorded shall be read by all other staff caring for the patient and co-ordinated so that the patient shall not be given conflicting advice. If any staff member disagrees with the advice or information given to the patient, that disagreement shall be taken up with the physician in charge of the case.

25. If any advice is given by telephone, that fact shall be noted in the record noting the time.

26. If further tests or opinions arise, which differ from the advice previously given to the patient, the patient and any other healthcare providers involved in the care of the patient shall be advised and the details of the advice shall be recorded.

27. Every member of the medical staff, after carrying out a medical, surgical or diagnostic procedure, shall leave instructions for the care of the patient with the staff and for patients and their home caregivers.

28. All members of the medical staff shall make themselves available following any medical, surgical or diagnostic procedure to discuss the procedure and to advice the patient and family.

29. Members of the medical staff shall ensure that instructions and advice given orally to other members of the staff and the patient and family shall not conflict with any written instructions or advice.

Policy 5.2: Record Keeping, Handling and Maintenance — Handwritten Records	
Objective:	*The purpose of this policy is to ensure the accuracy and effectiveness of the written communication system within healthcare sites, institutions and among healthcare providers. This objective will aim to lessen the risk of patient injury and maintain quality standards of care. It will also provide recorded evidence of those standards and evidence as to whether those standards have been met. If the standards have been met, the record will be the primary source of evidence in the defence of litigation. The record also provides information which when analyzed can be the basis of quality improvement programs, and staff education to avoid failures in the maintenance of standards.* *This policy is based on an address by Lorne E. Rozovsky and Noela J. Inions before the Canadian Health Record Association in Toronto on June 7, 2003 and from "Canadian Health Information: A Practical Legal and Risk Management Guide", 3rd ed. by Rozovsky and Inions (Markham, ON: Butterworths, 2002).*
Application:	*This policy applies to every person making any handwritten record or communication within the institution, office or clinic.*
Cross-References:	P5.3
Policies:	All staff recording and using information in the records shall abide by the following guidelines. 1. Write legibly. 2. Write accurately. 3. Write concisely. 4. Record events chronologically. 5. Record information immediately or as soon as possible. 6. Do not rush. 7. Read the entry immediately after making it. 8. Do not assume that those who will be reading the handwritten information are familiar with the handwriting.

9. Do not assume that everyone reading the information is familiar with the subject matter.

10. Do not assume that you can always read your own handwriting with accuracy.

11. All entries in the record must be made by the person who was directly involved in the event recorded.

12. All entries must be signed.

13. The person who made the entry must sign all entries.

14. Write in ink.

15. Try not to change pens in the midst of writing an entry in the record.

16. Use uniform terminology throughout the facility.

17. Use uniform abbreviations throughout the facility.

18. Establish a uniform system of handwriting numerals.

19. Encourage the use of handwritten block letters rather than cursive.

20. Use a uniform system of recording information throughout the organization.

21. Correct errors openly and honestly.

22. Do not add editorial comments, other than professional opinions on the material being recorded.

23. So that misinterpretation of handwritten numbers does not occur, the following numbers are to be written as indicated:

1 -	*1*	not	*1*	not	/	not	*1*
1	*4*	not	*4*	not	*4*		
7 -	*7*	not	*7*	not	*7*		
8 -	*8*	not	*8*	not	*8*		
0 -	*O*	not	*0*	not	*2*		
Point -	•	not	o	not	,		

24. In writing a decimal, it is to be written as a point, and not as a small circle.

25. A number which contains a comma, must have the comma as a comma and not as a decimal,

and should be small enough so as not to be confused with a numeral.

26. Block printing is to be preferred over cursive with letters being spaced so as not to run into each other.

27. While block letters are to be preferred, if cursive is used, lower case letters are to be written in the manner indicated.

b *b* r *r*

c *c* s *s*

e *e* t *t*

i *i* u *u*

k *k* v *v*

o *o* x *x*

30. Any record used in the healthcare system is a communication which means that it must be written so that it can be communicated.

Policy 5.3: Record Keeping, Handling and Maintenance — How to Complete Forms

Objective:	*The effectiveness of standardized forms as part of the patient record or to ensure that predetermined standards are met depends not only on their design, but that they are completed and used as intended. This is particularly important since one of the main purposes of a form is to provide consistency throughout the institution, organization or practice. A further purpose is to ensure that certain set standards are met. The failure to correctly complete a form may result in a subsequent failure to meet those standards, which may not only cause injury, but will also be evidence that there has been a failure and that negligence occurred.*
Application:	*All staff who are required to complete predesigned forms in the administration of various aspects of their patient care and other duties.*
Cross-References:	P5.2
Policies:	1. Complete forms exactly according to the instructions.
	2. Do not alter the set wording of a form.
	3. If a form cannot be completed as it is designed because of the fact situation presented, make a note on the form that it is "not applicable" or "N/A" and a further note advising the reader to see an attached note in which the correct information is noted, dated and signed.
	4. Do not leave any spaces blank. If they cannot be answered because they are not applicable, note "N/A".
	5. Complete all forms using BLOCK LETTERS that are absolutely clear and easy to read
	6. Any signatures must be followed by the name of the person signing in BLOCK LETTERS followed by their professional designation, *e.g.*, MD, RN, Ph.D, *etc.*, and their identification (ID) number.
	7. Dates must never be written entirely in numerals. Designate the day first in numerals, followed by the month as an abbreviation except for the shorter month designations, *e.g.*, Feb., June, July, Sep., *etc.*
	8. If a form is more than one page, every page must be initialled on the top right-hand corner.

9.   If a form consists of more than one page, the order of the pages must not be changed.

10. If an error is made on a form, the incorrect entry is to have a line drawn through it without obliterating it, and the correction added followed by the initial of the person signing the form and the date on which the correction was made. Do not make any attempt to erase the error nor to cover it up.

11. Any entry which consists of medical terminology or abbreviations shall conform to the list of terms and abbreviations to be used in the institution, organization or practice.

12. Do not use abbreviations in the completion of forms unless the form specifically states that this is permissible.

13. Complete forms only in black or blue pen. Do not use any other colour. Do not use pencil.

14. On completing a form, always read it over afterwards to check on its accuracy and to ensure that someone else, perhaps from a different department or discipline, can read the entries and understand them.

Policy 5.4:   Record Keeping, Handling and Maintenance — Patient Record Handling

Objective:	*One of the greatest risks of a professional negligence suit occurs not in the actual treatment or diagnosis aspect, but in the handling of the patient record. This risk can be diminished by following a strict procedure for everyone in the office or clinic who comes into contact with the patient and handles the record.*
	There should be no deviation in the procedure either by any individual or within the organization. The procedure should become second nature to everyone. It then becomes the standard, which will not only assist in reducing the risk of liability arising from the handling of the record, but becomes the standard against which any complaint will be compared.
	The purpose of the procedure is to avoid situations in which the record is not read, or that the record of a patient is confused with the record of another patient, or that the information required is not in the record.
Application:	*This policy is designed for a patient seen by a physician in a private practice or clinic, and may be adapted to similar situations involving other health professionals including dentists, physiotherapists and various mental health therapists.*
Cross-References:	F5
Policies:	1. Immediately before a patient meets with the doctor (and not after the patient has entered), the record must be pulled from the file and given directly to the doctor. If the patient does not show, the record should not be given to the doctor unless it is flagged for review and possible follow-up.
	2. The person who actually pulls the file shall make certain that the file is in fact the file of the patient to be seen, and not a patient with a similar name, such as another member of the same family, or someone with the same name.
	3. Before the patient's file is placed on the doctor's desk, all other files should be removed. This will avoid confusion with other files and prevent a patient from seeing the file names of other patients, thus breaching confidentiality.
	4. Before reading the file, the doctor shall confirm that

	the file is of the patient who is to be seen.
	5. A cover sheet shall be attached to the outside of all patient files indicating whether all information expected has been received, and whether any further information has yet to be filed.
	6. A patient shall not be seen by a doctor until the doctor has had an opportunity to review the file.
	7. While the doctor is reviewing a file, there shall be no telephone calls or other interruptions.
	8. While a file is being reviewed, no other material is to be read or examined, either written or on a computer monitor unless it pertains to the file being reviewed.
	9. In reviewing a patient's file, particular attention shall be paid to current drugs, allergies, conditions that may affect current or further treatment, and any action which should have been taken prior to the current visit.
	10. In reviewing a file, conclusions or opinions shall be based solely on the information in the file, and not on memory. If by chance, it appears that information may be absent from the file, a note is to be made for follow-up.
	11. Special attention must be paid to any information in the file which may require follow-up. A note shall be made as to the follow-up required with an additional note on the exterior cover sheet so that a diary entry may be made to ensure that the necessary action is taken.
	12. When any patient is moved from one department or service to another within an institution, the patient's records shall accompany the patient. A record shall be made of the transfer and maintained in the department or services from which the patient was transferred.

Policy 5.5:   Record Keeping, Handling and Maintenance — Retention, Storage and Disposal of Health Information

Objective:	*The purpose of this policy is to make certain that a mechanism is in place so that relevant information is available for continued or future care or treatment of current and previous patients. The goal is to maintain accuracy and accessibility of information. Its purpose is also to protect the legal position of the institution and its staff from litigation arising from the loss of information or the improper dissemination of a patient's health information, and to maintain information which may be needed as long as the institution and its staff may be subject to litigation. For a more complete explanation of the legal implications of this policy see "Canadian Health Information: A Practical Legal and Risk Management Guide", 3rd ed., by Lorne E. Rozovsky and Noela J. Inions (Markham, ON: Butterworths Canada, 2002), c. 5.*
Application:	*Director and staff of health information management, risk management staff, director of security.*
Cross-References:	P2.4; F32; F33; F34
Policies:	1. The director of health information management in conjunction with the director of security, the chief executive officer, the director of risk management and legal counsel shall establish and monitor a security system which will control the dissemination or theft of patient health information from the institution, while allowing the dissemination of the information for the proper care and treatment of patients, and the maintenance of the institution according to appropriate standards and legal requirements. 2. The security policy may designate staff positions that are permitted access to patient health information and those which are not, including that information which may be accessed and that which may not. 3. The director of health information after consultation with the heads of all clinical departments and services, and legal counsel, shall establish retention periods during which designated categories of information shall be retained.

	4.	A policy and procedure may also be established for the transference of health information from one format to another once the retention period has expired.
	5.	All staff shall be required as a condition of employment or staff privileges to sign a confidentiality agreement with respect to patient health information.
	6.	The director of health information management after consultation with legal counsel, the director of security and the chief executive officer shall establish a mechanism for the destruction of health information records with specific attention to the prevention of breach of security of the records en route to and during destruction, and to ensure that the destruction of the information is totally effective.
	7.	A record shall be maintained documenting the expiration of the required retention period, and the date, time and name, signature of the person supervising the destruction of the records, and a record of which documents have been destroyed.

Policy 6.1:   Patient Safety — Use of Medical, Surgical and Other Devices

Objective:	*Patient safety frequently depends not only on the judgement and ability of individual healthcare providers, but also on medical, surgical and other devices and equipment. This policy is designed to establish a regimen that will limit the possibility of patient injury being caused through the use of devices and equipment, and to manage the risk of liability as a result of injury or allegations of such injury. In this policy, the word "device" is used to refer to any equipment or device for any provision of healthcare diagnosis, care or treatment.*
Application:	*This policy applies to all members of the medical staff and staff members generally who are called to use any medical, surgical or other device or equipment in the performance of their duties, and all members of the engineering and computer services departments.*
Cross-References:	
Policies:	1. No member of the medical staff nor any employee of the institution shall use any device without having received permission by the head of the individual's department to use the device.
	2. No permission shall be given for the use of any device under this policy unless the person being given the permission shows evidence of having been trained to use the device, and is competent in its use.
	3. At any time, permission to use such devices may be contingent on further training.
	4. No device may be brought by any member of staff onto the premises of the institution for use in the diagnosis, care or treatment of patients without specific approval by executive, medical director and risk manager.
	5. Any indication that a device is not working correctly shall be taken out of service immediately and reported to the appropriate administrative officer.
	6. In any situation in which a device is taken out of service, immediate action shall be taken to have the patient transferred to another facility that can supply

that device, or the procedure may continue with the use of an alternative device in its absence, but only following the written approval of the medical director.

7.   No staff member shall use any device without being trained in its use, and only if its use is clearly within the bounds of the member's professional licensing, and in the case of a member of the medical staff, within the bounds of the privileges held by that staff member.

8.   No staff member shall attempt to repair or alter any device, without the direct involvement of the hospital engineering department.

9.   Devices which have been designated by the manufacturer for single use only shall be discarded after one use and not re-used.

10.   A program shall be established to monitor the use of all devices in order to determine their efficacy and to make certain that the devices are being used by staff within their competency to use such devices, and that the devices are being used for the appropriate patients in appropriate circumstances.

11.   Failure to meet these standards shall be reported to the appropriate professional committee, and action with respect to continuing education, or disciplinary action shall be taken.

12.   Sales and other representatives of manufacturers or distributors of devices may be permitted in attendance when a device is being used with the permission of the patient, but shall not be permitted to use such devices on any patient.

Policy 7.1: Incidents, Errors and Complaints — Reporting Incidents and Errors	
Objective:	*This policy is designed to ensure that incidents and errors are reported, analyzed and reviewed for the purpose of avoiding or at least lessening such occurrences in the future. The collection of such information is also useful in the defence of any litigation that might arise, or in the analysis of such occurrences in order to assist in the settlement of any claims in order to avoid litigation.*
Application:	*The policy applies to all members of the staff, risk management staff, administrative staff and legal counsel.*
Cross-References:	
Policies:	**Incidents and Errors**

<table>
<tr><td></td><td>

1.   All staff members, employees, trustees or volunteers are obligated to report to the risk manager any suspected violation of these policies, or any suspected unprofessional, unethical, or illegal conduct in the institution or involving the work of the institution.

2.   The position of any person who files such a report under section 1 of this policy shall not be jeopardized by the filing of such a report, unless it is clearly shown that such a report is filed frivolously or with malicious intent.

3.   The report shall be recorded by the risk manager in the prescribed form and signed by the person reporting.

4.   The report of the matter shall be maintained by the risk manager who shall investigate the matter and may consult with the CEO and legal counsel.

5.   Incidents and errors shall be compiled and analyzed by the director of risk management in conjunction with such other staff members as may be appropriate in order to determine the cause of such incidents or errors, and to make recommendations to the chief executive officer and the board as to how these incidents or errors may be lessened in terms of risk and severity, or eliminated.

Complaints

Any staff member having a complaint about any other staff
</td></tr>
</table>

	member, if the matter cannot be resolved between them, shall pass on the complaint to the immediate supervisor or department head of the complainant. If a resolution is not forthcoming, the complainant may take the complaint to that person's immediate supervisor. If the complaint involves an immediate risk to the life or health of any person, or to property, the complaint may be made to the administrator on duty, or in extreme cases to security staff. All complaints shall be documented by the person receiving them with the advice of the complainant.

Policy 7.2:	Incidents, Errors and Complaints — How to Handle Complaints
Objective:	*The purpose of this policy is to remove or at least lessen antagonism arising from the way in which a complaint regarding the care of a patient is handled. The aim is to improve what may have been a damaged personal relationship so that it does not escalate into litigation or a disciplinary complaint. The handling of complaints by patients and their families can be difficult especially if the person complaining, whether a patient or someone on behalf of a patient, is emotionally upset. The method of handling the complaint may have an effect on whether legal action is subsequently taken, or how uncooperative a person is if legal action is taken. Many people become antagonistic if they are given the impression that no one cares, and that no one is really sorry. At the same time, care must be taken not to say anything that could be taken as an admission of liability without the prior advice of legal counsel.*
Application:	*Complaints or any indication that a patient or family may be dissatisfied should be handled by a person specifically designated to handle complaints. However, the policy applies to all staff members who are under an obligation to put this policy into activation.*
Cross-References:	F36
Policies:	1. Respond immediately. If you are aware that someone has a complaint make certain that you meet with him or her personally and as quickly as possible. 2. Ask the complainant if you could take notes, and explain that you want to make sure that you have an accurate and detailed account of the complaint so that it can be investigated properly. 3. Listen attentively. Do not interrupt the person complaining. Before starting, ask the complainant if he or she minds if you interrupt occasionally to ask questions to make sure that you understand and that you have an accurate account of what you are being told. 4. When accusations are made, do not be defensive, even if the accusations are malicious, offensive and untrue. Do not argue, and do not let yourself be

pulled into an argument. Express understanding and empathy, but do not patronize. Do not say, "I am sorry you feel that way", which implies that you are sorry about their feelings but not about what happened to them. Do not say, "I understand how you feel", since their response will invariably be "No, you do not", which may result in a confrontation.

5. Do not respond to the complaint by blaming someone else or making excuses.

6. Do not use an aggressive tone of voice.

7. Look directly at the person when discussing the complaint.

8. Take notes during any conversation regarding the complaint, and advise those attending that you are doing so in order to make certain that you have an accurate record of their complaint.

9. During the conversation or when it is over, review your notes and ask questions to make certain that you have an accurate record of the complaint.

10. The complaint is to be discussed with the director of risk management and legal counsel for advice on further handling.

11. When all facts have been gathered it is important that the health professionals and the complaints officer express their sorrow as to what happened and to apologize. This is not an admission of liability, but a full explanation of what happened and an expression of regret will frequently reduce the risk of litigation or other legal action, or at least allow discussions regarding settlement of any claim to take place in a more productive manner.

12. Finally, ask what the complainant wants. Do not ask in an aggressive or defensive manner. Phrase it in a more roundabout way such as "What do you think we can do about this, not only to help you but to prevent this from happening to other patients."

13. If you are in a position to do so, explain what steps you will take. Be very careful not to promise to do something or have the institution do something which it may not be able to do, either administratively or

legally. You may have to advise the complainant that you are not sure of what can be done but you will find out and report back. Say how long this might take, and be good to your word.

14.   If there is a delay in responding to the complaint, advise the person complaining. Never leave the impression that the matter has been either forgotten or dropped.

15.   If you are able to, or on the follow-up visit, advise what the alternatives are.

16.   Put everything you have been told by the complainant, and everything that has been discovered during the subsequent investigation in a separate complaint record.

17.   Do not put the details of the complaint investigation in the patient's record, though a cross-reference to the fact that there is a complaint file is important.

18.   Refer the entire matter to the risk manager, and if there is any indication of patient injury, or potential legal action, the risk manager is to refer the matter to legal counsel and to the insurer.

19.   The staff caring for that patient involved should be informed about the complaint and instructed not to comment on it, unless instructed otherwise by the CEO or risk manager or whoever has the authority over the handling of complaints.

Policy 7.3: Incidents, Errors and Complaints — Notification of Patients of Errors or Accidents	
Objective:	*The purpose of this policy is to ensure that errors which might conceivably affect one or more patients are immediately communicated to these patients in order to minimize any risks to the health of those patients, and to lessen the risks of liability by taking all reasonable steps to lessen patient injury. Otherwise, even if human or technical error or occurrence is not to blame, there is a duty on the healthcare provider to take reasonable steps to lessen the possibility of patient injury.*
Application:	*Setting this policy into place should be co-ordinated by the risk manager with the co-operation of the medical director, the chief executive officer, and the head of the the department or departments which may have been involved. The health information manager should also be involved in order to set up a look-back system in order to find the names and contact information of patients who may have been affected.*
Cross-References:	F32; F33; F36
Policies:	1. In the case of an error or accident in the use of equipment, drugs, or the facilities, which could potentially cause or have caused harm to patients, a written notification shall be sent to all patients, or their representatives.
	2. The notification under this policy shall be signed by the chief executive officer.
	3. Any notification under this policy shall be reviewed by legal counsel and by the risk manager prior to its approval.
	4. A notification under this policy shall include:
	a. advice as to the occurrence without any speculation as to how or why it occurred, nor shall any accusations as to blame be included;
	b. an apology without any admission of liability;
	c. the potential risk of harm;
	d. symptoms that should be noted;
	e. what action the patient should take whether symptoms arise or not;

	f.	any activities, drugs or medications that patient should avoid;
	g.	who the patient should contact, under what conditions, and how quickly the contact should be made.
	5.	A copy of the notification shall be sent to the patient's primary care physician.
	6.	A copy of the notification shall be placed in the patient's file.
	7.	A record of all those to whom a notification has been sent shall be maintained by the risk manager.

Policy 7.4: Incidents, Errors and Complaints — Challenging Treatment Orders	
Objective:	*It is recognized that when a patient is being cared for by a number of individuals whether they are of the same discipline or not, there will occasionally be disagreements in decisions that are made. It is important for the care of any patient being cared for by a number of people, that the patient has the benefit of all opinions. It is also recognized that the primary caregiver or the head of the team has to make the final decision. It must however, be made after consideration is given to other opinions especially from other disciplines that can bring to the decision-making process information and knowledge which the primary caregiver may not be aware. Failure to obtain these other opinions, and to communicate them to the other members of the team, may be considered as negligence if the patient is injured as a result. Accurate recording of the so-called challenge to a decision is essential to make certain that it is communicated, and that there is a record, which can be used in evidence that such a challenge did take place and was considered.*
Application:	*It is extremely important that all members of the staff regardless of discipline accept the fact that their opinion may be challenged and that they can challenge the opinions of others. It must also be understood that these challenges should not be taken as an attempt to attack or oppose the authority or judgment, but to contribute to the decision-making process. All members must also recognize that their challenges may not necessarily be accepted but that they have fulfilled their duty to the patient by making them.* *To make certain that this policy is in effect, all members of the staff on joining the staff must be acquainted with it, and must be reminded from time to time.*
Cross-References:	
Policies:	1. Any staff member who is responsible for caring and treating a patient who disagrees with any treatment order shall discuss that order with the individual who issued it, and seek confirmation, retraction or alteration of the order. 2. Under ordinary circumstances no staff member shall

unilaterally disregard, alter or otherwise contravene any care or treatment order given by another member of the staff regardless of discipline.

3.   If a staff member wishes to discuss an order under this policy with another staff member who issued the order and the staff member who issued the order is not available, the discussion shall be held with the supervisor of that staff member or in the case of a member of the medical staff, with the head of the member's department or the medical director.

4.   In an emergency situation if the carrying out of an order is likely to cause immediate injury, a staff member who is authorized may retract or alter the order. This policy shall only be implemented if it would be unreasonable to consult with the person who gave the order, or such other person as required under this policy.

5.   Any action taken under section 7.4.4 of this policy shall be reported as quickly as possible to the supervisor or in the case of a member of the medical staff to the medical director.

6.   Any action taken under this policy shall be recorded noting the reason for the action.

Policy 8.1: Public Relations — Media and Press Policy	
Objective:	*All contact with the press shall be handled with great care from both a legal and risk management point of view. Information about the institution, the board of trustees, the relationship between the corporation and any other organization or government body, or about any patient or the patient's family or friends, any employee, any member of the medical or dental staff, or any volunteer, or anyone having any contract or relationship with the institution or any person or body associated with it, shall not be divulged except according to this policy.*
	The risks involved in divulging information to the press include breach of privacy, breach of contract, and libel and slander. Information, whether correct or not, can also affect the relationship between the institution and the community, government, other institutions and trade and professional associations and unions.
	The media and press policy shall be circulated to all members of the press within the community served by the organization, as well as to all board members, staff and employees and volunteers. Because of changes in staffing, the policy is to be circulated at least twice a year.
Application:	*This policy applies to all medical and other staff, members of the board, and volunteers.*
Cross-References:	
Policies:	1. **Philosophy.** All press releases, press interviews and public statements made on behalf of the .... (organization) shall be in the spirit of the (*e.g.*, religious, if appropriate) tradition and philosophy, in good taste and shall not contravene any policy of the board of trustees, nor shall any press releases, press interview or public statement express any opinion or promote any cause or idea except within the spirit of this section.
	2. **Reputation.** Exceptional care shall be taken in the public statements that could affect the reputation of the organization and its relations with other organizations, government and the public.
	3. **Prior review.** All public statements issued in

writing shall receive prior review by the executive director, the public relations officer, legal counsel and the person in charge of the department directly implicated by the statement, to insure accuracy and to avoid legal and other unintended implications.

4. **Oral press statements.** No trustee, employee, or member of staff shall make any statements to the press without obtaining the approval of the executive director.

5. **Policies and positions.** No public statement concerning a policy or position of the organization shall be made except with the approval of the board or the executive director.

6. **Restrictions.** From time to time, the executive director or the board may place restrictions on the issuing of written press statements or the making of oral statements to the press.

7. **Public relations officer**

   a. All requests by the press for statements, interviews, opinions or comments shall be referred to the public relations officer, or the executive director.

   b. All local press and media organizations shall be informed as to the name and contact information for the public relations officer of the organization.

   c. When referring the press to the spokesperson for the organization, no comment or opinion regarding the query or any other matter shall be made.

8. **Release of personal information**

   a. No public statement concerning any former, current or prospective patient, client, employee, medical or dental staff member, or member of the board shall be made without the consent of the person identified, except on the specific directions of the executive director following consultation with legal counsel.

   b. Where the consent of a person under this section

to the release of information is not possible owing to the lack of mental or physical capability, legal incapacity or death, consent may be given by the legally authorized representative of such person.

c.   Consent or refusal to the release of information under this section shall be documented.

d.   Any person consenting to the release of information under this section on behalf of any other person shall be required to given evidence of being authorized to give such consent.

9.   **Definition of a patient's condition**

a.   The condition of a patient or a former patient may be described in any oral or written statement to the press as follows, and the press are to be given a copy of the following definitions.

b.   "Good" means that the patient is conscious and comfortable, vital signs are stable and are within normal limits.

c.   "Fair" means that the patient is conscious, vital signs give no cause for concern and prognosis is favourable, but the patient is uncomfortable or may have minor complications.

d.   "Serious" means that the patient is acutely ill, vital signs may be either unstable or outside normal limits, prognosis is questionable, but improvement is probable.

e.   "Critical" means that vital signs are unstable and not within normal limits, prognosis is questionable, there are major complications and death may be imminent, but improvement is possible.

10.   **Licensed or accredited.** The terms "licensed" or "accredited" shall only be used in a statement to the press with the designation of the licensing or accrediting body.

11.   **Photographs.** No person shall take or be permitted to take on the premises or at any activity held by or under the auspices of the organization any photo-

	graph, motion picture, video film or television picture, or any other electronic, mechanical or audio-recording, except on the authorization of the executive director and the consent of any person being photographed or recorded.

PART III

FORMS

PATIENTS — Admissions/Assessments/Discharges/Exits

Form 1: Patient's Advice Sheet

Objective: *The purpose of the form is to set a standard by which patients, their families and their physicians or their healthcare institutions can relate. Specifically, it puts the patient on notice as to what the provider can and cannot do, thus assisting the patient in obtaining a proper standard of care, and not seeking or expecting services which cannot be provided. This will hopefully lower the risk of liability based on a reliance which is unrealistic and provoke litigation when that reliance cannot be fulfilled. The form also advises the patient that some of the care belongs with the patient and not with the provider.*

Application: *Every new patient is to be given this form, and from time to time, at least annually, all patients are to be given the form as updated.*

(Name of Institution)
Patient's Advice Sheet

Note to Patient: The practice of medicine is not an exact science. It involves scientific judgment but also varies with each individual, both physically and mentally, and the circumstances in which they live. Therefore, there is no "quick fix", and there is no guarantee. However, to increase the possibilities of successful treatment, the patient and the doctor must work together.

The following guidelines will help us provide you with quality medical care:

1. Before coming to the doctor, write out a list of questions, symptoms and concerns.

2. Make a list of all current medications, including dosages and strength. Include both prescription and non-prescription drugs regardless of who prescribed them. Leave a copy of the list with the doctor, and with your spouse or person you live with, and keep a copy in your wallet or purse at all times. If there is any change, amend the list, date it, and give a copy to the same people who have the previous list. Include on this list a separate category of all drug, food and product allergies.

3. Advise the doctor of any religious or cultural issues that might affect any care or treatment.

4. Keep a binder at home with all of your medical records, and reports, and keep it updated.

5. Do not discontinue any treatments or medications without first consulting your doctor.

6. If there are any side effects from any treatment or medication, advise your doctor immediately.

7. Compile a list of all surgeries you have had for your doctor along with when they were performed, and a list of serious diseases you have had, and any chronic conditions.

8. If you are being treated by more than one physician, all of your physicians should be advised of the name, address, telephone number and specialty of all of the other physicians.

9. If you have any advance directive, or any document which limits the treatment which you are willing to accept, give your doctor a copy.

10. Advise your doctor of what you do for a living, what you do when off work, and any activities that might be the cause of physical or medical problems.

Patient's Name: _____ Page (1/1)

PATIENTS — Admissions/Assessments/Discharges/Exits

Form 2: Patient Information

Objective: *The purpose of this form is to protect patient safety by insuring that the correct care and treatment is given to the right patient (or resident) and to highlight conditions which will provide warnings in the provision of care and treatment. This form is also designed to provide information which is to assist in communication with the patient or resident.*

Application: *The information on this form shall be added to any further information which the particular institution may require. Prior to meeting a patient or resident, or providing care or treatment, this form shall be read by the healthcare provider involved. The information on this form shall be compared with any other documentation to make certain that there are no inconsistencies. Any inconsistencies shall be immediately reported to the supervisor in charge and to the health records department for review and correction. The healthcare provider shall not make changes in this form or any other document as a result of inconsistencies without following this procedure. No care or treatment shall be given in contravention of any contraindications noted except with the specific signed approval of the attending physician having been notified of the contraindication.*

(Name of Institution)		
Patient Information		
Name:	_____ _____ _____ (last) (first) (middle)	
Patient No.:		
Date of Birth:	_____ / _____ / _____ (yyyy) (mm) (dd)	
OHIP:		
SIN:		
Address:		
Mother tongue:		
Language ordinarily used:		
Other languages:	(1) _____ (speaking level)	_____ (understanding level)
	(2) _____ (speaking level)	_____ (understanding level)
Allergies:	Medications: Food: Smells: Chemicals (including cleaning preparations):	

	Other materials (*e.g.*, latex): _____ _____
Personality traits, or mental characteristics which might affect care or treatment: _____ _____	
Physical disabilities which may affect care or treatment:	Sight: _____ _____ Hearing: _____ _____ Speech: _____ _____ Mobility: _____ _____

Form filled out by: _____

Date: _____

PATIENTS — Admissions/Assessments/Discharges/Exits
Form 3: Patient's Authorization to Disclose Information

Objective: *The purpose of this form is to advise the patient or a substitute when the patient is either legally or mentally not competent to give such authorization that it is the patient's right to authorize disclosure of information held by the healthcare provider, or not to authorize its disclosure, and to provide documentation for the healthcare provider as to what the patient or the patient's substitute has done.*

Application: *This form should be presented to the patient or the patient's substitute at the time of admission. It is usually advisable to give the patient or the substitute an opportunity to review the authorization if any condition or information regarding the patient's condition changes.*

Cross-references: P5.1

(Name of Institution)		
Patient Information		
Patient Name:	 _____ _____ _____ (last) (first) (middle)		
Patient No.:	 _____		
Date of Birth:	_____ / _____ / _____ (yyyy) (mm) (dd)		
OHIP:	 _____		
SIN:	 _____		
Address:	 _____		
Telephone:	 _____ _____ _____ (day) (evening) (cell)		

I hereby authorize _____

(name of institution, clinic or practitioner)

to release all information indicated below related to the above named patient to:

Name (institution, clinic, provider, or individual): _____

Address: _____

_____

Telephone No.: _____ _____

(check those desired)

Summary   ☐

Discharge summary   ☐

Diagnosis results related to condition_____ ☐

Care provided during the following period _____ ☐

Any documentation as requested by recipient _____

2.   Notwithstanding the above authorization, the following information or documentation is not to be released: _____

_____

_____

....

Name of authorized person: _____   _____ _____
                                                  (last)   (first)   (middle)

If not patient, indicate relationship to patient: _____

Address: _____

Telephone: (day) _____ (evening) _____(cell) _____

E-mail: _____

Identification of authorization and confirmation of authority by: _____

Telephone: _____

Signature: _____

Name: _____

Date: _____

PATIENTS — Admissions/Assessments/Discharges/Exits

Form 4: Patient Property List and Release

Objective: *The purpose of this form is ensure that there is an accurate record of any property given to the institution by the patient (or resident), in order to avoid disputes.*

Application: *It is important that the property received by the patient is immediately in the presence of the patient and a witness be placed in a security box and sealed. The security box shall be immediately taken to a secure location by two employees of the institution and locked. Neither the box nor any of the property shall at any time be left out without security.*

(Name of Institution)

Patient Property List and Release

Patient's Name:	_____ _____ _____ (last) (first) (middle)
Date of Birth:	_____ / _____ / _____ (yyyy) (mm) (dd)
OHIP:	
SIN:	
Patient No.:	
Date of admission:	
Department:	
Room No.:	

I, _____ of _____ ,
  (last)   (first)   (middle)   (address)

assume all responsibility for property brought with me to the (name of institution) on the following list while I am a patient in the (name of institution).

I, hereby release the (name of institution), its medical staff and all employees and volunteers for the loss of, or damage to, any of the articles on the list regardless of the cause of such loss or damage.

List of items:

Circle if applicable and add brief description

- Contact lenses: _____
- Dentures: _____
- Glasses: _____
- Hearing aid: _____

- Jewelry: _____
  - Bracelet(s) _____
  - Earring(s) _____
  - Necklace _____
  - Pin(s) _____
  - Watch _____
- Purse: _____
- Wallet: _____
- Credit cards: _____
- Cash: _____
- Clothing (list): _____

  _____

  _____

- Medications (list): _____

  _____

  _____

- Others: _____

  _____

  _____

_____

Received by: _____
                 (print name and signature)

Signature of patient or representative: _____
Date and time: _____

Returned by: _____
                 (print name and signature)

Date and signature: _____
Received by patient or representative: _____
                              (print name and signature)

PATIENTS — Admissions/Assessments/Discharges/Exits

Form 5: Special Handling and Alerts

Objective: *While consistent practice in the handling of patients assists in maintaining a predetermined level of care, there are many situations in which standard practice may be injurious to individual patients due to individual medical circumstances or characteristics unique to that patient. Failure to recognize these situations and to act on them may result in patient injury and potential liability of the healthcare provider and the health institution. This form is designed to bring these situations to the attention of any person coming into contact with the patient.*

Application: *When the patient's record is compiled, the attending physician or other person compiling the information has a duty to ask appropriate questions which may result in answers requiring special handling of the patient. The alert form with this information should be placed on the outside cover of the file, so that the person reading the file is immediately aware that standard practice must not be followed in some instances. No action should be taken in contravention of the special handling requirements, except if the attending physician specifically requires it.*

Cross-references: P3.2; P5.1; P5.3; P5.4

(Name of Institution)

SPECIAL HANDLING & ALERTS

Patient's Name:

Patient No.:

(check as applicable)

- **DRUG ALLERGIES:**
- **FOOD ALLERGIES:**
- **OTHER PRODUCT ALLERGIES:**
- **CONTAGIOUS (details):**
- **OTHER CONDITIONS (*e.g.*, epileptic, dementia, *etc.*):**

CONFIDENTIAL Do not discuss with:

Exception: If there is a medical or other reason not to follow standard practice when any of the above situations arise, note the date, time, action taken and reasons for the practice not being followed:

Attending physician (signature) _____

Name: _____

Date:_____   Time: _____

SPECIAL RISK MANAGEMENT HANDLING:

(note date, time and name of person to whom information was referred)

- **Refer to insurer**
- **Refer to lawyer**
- **Refer to risk manager**
- **Notify security**

PATIENTS — Admissions/Assessments/Discharges/Exits

Form 6: Missed Appointments

Objective: *In many instances patients make appointments either on their own initiative or on the recommendation of their physician or other healthcare professional, but do not keep the appointments. The patient may not appreciate the seriousness of his or her situation, nor that failing to seek medical attention may result in injury. If the referring healthcare professional knows or ought to have known that the failure of the patient to seek care, treatment or advice could cause injury and that the patient had not been informed of this, the argument may be made that the healthcare professional is negligent in taking reasonable steps to prevent this from occurring.*

Application: *This form is to be an integral part of the appointment process. While the patient on making the appointment should be told by a healthcare professional of the importance of keeping the appointment, this form deals with the situation when a patient misses an appointment. It records the reasonable efforts made by the healthcare provider to prevent patient injury. It would be completed as soon as it is noted that a patient did not keep an appointment. It would then trigger various actions which must be recorded. This will prove to be the evidence that all reasonable steps have been taken to prevent patient injury. This form when complete is to be placed in patient's file.*

Cross-references: P3.4

(Name of Institution)

Missed Appointments

Patient's Name:	_____ _____ _____ (last) (first) (middle)
Patient Number:	_____
Telephone:	_____ _____ _____ (day) (evening) (cell)
Date and time of appointment missed:	_____ _____ (date) (time)
Telephone follow-up #1:	_____ _____ Answered: ☐ (name of caller) (date and time of call) No response: ☐
Telephone follow-up #2 (if no response to follow-up #1):	_____ _____ Answered: ☐ (name of caller) (date and time of call) No response: ☐

File pulled and referred to physician by:

                                            _____   _____
                                                 (name)   (date)

Action required: (physician's instructions):

_____

_____

_____

Action taken by:

                         _____   _____
                                     (name)   (date)

Advice to patient requesting rebooking

Check if applicable and provide date:

☐   Telephone contact at numbers on records: _____.
                                                                    (date)
☐   E-mail contact at numbers on records: _____.
                                                                (date)
☐   Telephone contacts with persons listed on patient record: _____.
                                                                                              (date)
☐   If no contact can be made, the patient shall be contacted by
         registered priority mail to contact the institution noting the major
         risks of leaving the institution: _____.
                                                        (date)
☐   If patient is considered a danger to himself or others, police have
         been advised: _____.
                                    (date)

Patient's Name: _____ Page (2/2)

PATIENTS — Admissions/Assessments/Discharges/Exits

Form 7: Home Care Assessment

Objective: *The purpose of this form is make certain that patients or residents are not placed in a home care situation whereby there might be injury because of home care being inappropriate considering the patient's physical, medical or mental circumstances, and the circumstances of the home in which they might be placed. To improperly place an individual may be considered as negligence if such injury is reasonably foreseeable.*

Application: *This form is to be completed as evidence that a professional assessment has been undertaken to determine whether an individual can be appropriately cared for in his or her own home with the staff available to the home care agency. Such an assessment must be designed to lower the risk of injury to the patient, and potential liability to the home care agency.*

Cross-references: P5.1

(Name of Institution)		
Home Care Assessment — form to be completed by the assessor		
Patient's Name:	_____ _____ _____ (last)　　　　　(first)　　　　　(middle)	
Patient Number:	_____	
Date of Birth:	_____ / _____ / _____ (yyyy)　(mm)　(dd)	
OHIP:	_____	
SIN:	_____	
Address:	_____	
Telephone:	_____ _____ _____ (day)　　　　　(evening)　　　　(cell)	
Representa-tive (if any):	_____ Address: _____ _____ Telephone: _____ _____ _____ (day)　　　(evening)　　　(cell)	

What services will the patient need?

1. _____

2. _____

3. _____

4. _____

_____

Does the home care agency have the resources to provide these services under the conditions and at the times required by the client?
Y _____ N _____

If not, why not?

_____

_____

If the healthcare agency can provide these services to this particular patient in the location required, are there any restrictions which the home care agency must place upon its ability to provide these services?
Y _____ N _____

If yes, list those restrictions.

_____

_____

_____

What does the healthcare agency require in order to carry out these services for this particular patient at the particular location? List.

_____

_____

_____

Does the patient's physician approve of the home care services being given to this patient at this location with the restrictions that may be noted?
Y _____ N _____

Name of physician (or social worker): _____

Address:

_____

_____

Telephone:

_____

....

Name of home care agency: _____

Address: _____

_____

_____

Telephone:

_____

Name of agency representative: _____

....

Name of assessor: _____

Position: _____

Organization: _____

Address: _____

_____

Telephone: _____

_____   _____
Signature of assessor   Date of assessment

PATIENTS — Admissions/Assessments/Discharges/Exits

Form 8: Patient Discharge Instructions

Objective: *The purpose of this form is twofold. The first is to make certain that the patient has been given appropriate advice on discharge from either an in-patient facility or a course of out-patient treatment in order to prevent the patient from being injured by taking steps that might be injurious or failing to take action that is necessary for the preservation of the patient's health. The second purpose is to provide the healthcare institution with evidence of what was told to the patient so that if a lawsuit does take place, there is evidence of exactly what was given to the patient. This of course, does not offer defence protection if what the patient was told was improper or incomplete, and as a result the patient was injured.*

Application: *The information on this form should be discussed with the patient, and then presented to the patient, or the person who will be looking after the patient on discharge. It is important that the patient is given to understand that the information on the form is a written version of what has already been discussed orally. And that the form is completed in a legible manner, so that it can be easily read and understood. It is also important that the form be completed in clear, unambiguous and simple language that the average lay person can understand.*

(Name of Institution)

Patient Discharge Instructions

To the attending physician:

Re: Patient's Name: _____ _____   _____
                                    (last)   (first)   (middle)
Patient Number: _____

Date of discharge: _____ / _____ / _____
                                    (yyyy)   (mm)   (dd)

1. All records made during the patient's stay in the institution or during the course of treatment have been reviewed for accuracy and completeness.

2. All medications have been reviewed as part of a complete profile of the patient's condition, allergies and any other medications being taken.

3. A copy of this information sheet and a discharge summary has been sent to the patient's family physician.

4. This form has been completed by the attending physician.

_____

Print name of attending physician: _____

Signature of attending physician: _____

Date: _____

(Name of Institution)
Patient Discharge Instructions

To the patient:

Patient's Name: _____   _____   _____
               (last)   (first)   (middle)

Patient Number: _____

Date of discharge: _____ / _____ / _____
                (yyyy)   (mm)   (dd)

Institution: _____

Attending physician: _____

The information on this form is the same information which was discussed with you orally.

- It is important that you keep this form and follow the instructions exactly. Do not make any changes in the treatment advised or discontinued any of the treatment without first discussing it with your family physician.

- Give a copy of this form to your own physician.

- You have the right to ask any questions of your attending physician on being given this form.

- If you have any questions which arise after your discharge, do not hesitate to call your family physician.

1. Dates of treatment: _____

2. Diagnosis: _____

3. Details of treatment: _____

   _____

4. Attending physician: _____

5. Surgeon or other specialist. _____

6. Diagnosis on discharge: _____

   _____

7. Medications on discharge: _____

   _____

8. When to be taken: _____

9. How much to be taken (dosage): _____

10. Conditions under which to be taken (with food, with water, *etc.*):

_____

11. Risks of medication (including those unique to the patient):

_____

12. **WARNINGS:** What to do or not to do if any of the following takes place:

_____

13. Whether you can substitute these medications for generic medications:

_____

14. The risks of over-dosage or under-dosage:

_____

15. Other medications or foods **NOT** to be taken with these medications:

_____

16. What to do, if you take too much:

_____

17. What to do if you miss taking the medication or you take the incorrect amount:

_____

18. Can I split the tablet? Yes ___ No ___

19. Do I have to keep the medication in the refrigerator? Yes ___ No ___

20. These medications have been reviewed by the pharmacists as part of the entire profile of the patient's medications and any allergies that the patient may have.

(print name of pharmacist) _____

(signature of pharmacist) _____

Date _____

21. Allergies to medications or any other substances? Yes ____ No ____

PATIENTS — Admissions/Assessments/Discharges/Exits

Form 9: Temporary Absence

Objective: *The purpose of this form is to give the institution evidence of a voluntary absence and to release the institution from any liability related to missing or damaged property while the patient is absent, and to release the institution from liability for any injury to the patient during absence. However, this form does not remove liability on the part of the physician or the institution if it would be considered negligent to allow the patient to be absent.*

Application: *All patients should be advised on admission that they are not to leave the premises or in some cases not to leave the department or floor without notifying staff. If they have been advised that a temporary absence is permissible, this form should then be completed. It should be noted that if the patient was advised not to leave the institution, the form relating to leaving against medical advice should be completed.*

Cross-references: P3.4; P4.1.11; F10; F11

(Name of Institution)
Temporary Absence

I am temporarily leaving the (name of institution) with the permission of my attending physician, _____. I shall leave the facility at _____ a.m. on (date) _____, and return on (date) _____ no later than _____ p.m.

I understand that the (name of institution) assumes no responsibility for any of my personal property that I leave in the institution during my absence that I have not surrendered to the business office for safekeeping.

I also understand that I shall not hold the institution responsible for any harm that may occur to me during my absence.

(signature) _____

(print name) _____

(witness' signature) _____

(witness' name in print) _____

(date) _____

PATIENTS — Admissions/Assessments/Discharges/Exits

Form 10: Leaving Hospital Against Medical Advice

Objective: *The purpose of this form is to put the patient on notice that leaving hospital against medical advice may have serious medical consequences, and releases the hospital and its staff from any legal responsibility that it may have for injuries related to such departure. It also provides the institution with evidence that the patient did in fact leave against medical advice and was not discharged in the usual manner.*

Application: *For this form to be effective, it is imperative that the patient is informed of the potential consequences of leaving the institution. If the patient leaves without notifying any staff member, all reasonable efforts must be made to locate the patient and to advise him or her to return, and to give the advice on the consequences of not returning. If the patient refuses to sign this document that part of the form related to that situation must be completed. If the patient gives any indication of desiring to leave the institution before discharge, the attending physician shall be notified immediately to advise the patient on the consequences. At no time however, can the staff forcibly confine or hold the patient to prevent departure.*

Cross-references: P3.4; P4.1.11; F9

(Name of Institution)
Leaving Hospital Against Medical Advice

Patient's Name: _____   _____   _____
(last)   (first)   (middle)

Patient Number: _____

Date: _____

Room: _____

Attending physician: _____

PART A

To be completed after the patient has been advised of the potential risks of leaving the institution.

I, (patient's name) _____ have decided against the advice of my attending physician, _____, to leave (name of institution).

I have been advised by _____ of the risks of leaving the institution, including the following:

_____

_____

_____

and have been advised not to leave.

I hereby release (name of institution), its staff and my attending physician from any liability for any harm caused to me by my leaving under these circumstances.

Patient's signature: _____

Witness' signature: _____

PART B

To be completed if the patient leaves the institution before advice on leaving can be given.

(Patient's name) _____ has left the institution (check one) _____ without notifying any staff member, or _____ refusing to sign PART A of this form, and therefore was not advised of the potential risks of leaving the institution.

The following steps have been taken to notify the patient and to advise on the risks of leaving the institution: (check as appropriate noting date and time, and individual who attempted the contact (name, department and signature):

a.   Telephone contact at numbers on records: _____   _____
                                                    (date)   (time)

b.   E-mail contact at numbers on records: _____   _____
                                                (date)   (time)

c.   Telephone contacts with persons listed on
     patient record: _____   _____
                      (date)   (time)

d.   If no contact can be made, the patient shall be contacted by registered priority mail to contact the institution noting the major risks of leaving the institution: _____   _____
                                            (date)   (time)

e.   If patient is considered a danger to himself or others, police have been advised: _____   _____
                      (date)   (time)

Items checked:

☐   Telephone contact at numbers on records:

     Name of Contact: _____

     Person making contact (print): _____

     Signature: _____

     Date/time: _____   _____

☐   E-mail contact at numbers on records:

     Name of Contact: _____

     Person making contact (print): _____

     Signature: _____

     Date/time: _____

☐   Telephone contacts with persons listed on patient record:

Name of Contact: _____

Person making contact (print): _____

Signature: _____

Date/time: _____

☐   If no contact can be made, the patient shall be contacted by registered priority mail to contact the institution noting the major risks of leaving the institution:

Name of Contact: _____

Person making contact (print): _____

Signature: _____

Date/time: _____

☐   If patient is considered a danger to himself or others, police have been advised:

Name of Contact: _____

Person making contact (print): _____

Signature: _____

Date/time: _____

Patient's Name: _____ Page (3/3)

PATIENTS — Admissions/Assessments/Discharges/Exits

Form 11: Leaving Treatment Against Advice (non-hospital)

Objective: *The purpose of this form is to put the patient on notice that leaving treatment against healthcare provider's advice may have serious medical or health consequences, and releases the provider from any legal responsibility that the provider may have for injuries related to such departure. It also provides the provider with evidence that the patient did in fact leave against advice and was not discharged in the usual manner.*

Application: *This form may be used for non-hospital treatment situations such as physiotherapy clinics, mental health clinics, alcohol or drug rehabilitation centres, dental clinics or individual professional practices such as psychotherapy. For this form to be effective, it is imperative that the patient is informed of the potential consequences of leaving the treatment. If the patient leaves without notifying any staff member, all reasonable efforts must be made to locate the patient. The patient should be advised to return and informed of the consequences of not returning. If the patient refuses to sign this document that part of the form related to that situation must be completed. If the patient gives any indication of desiring to leave before discharge, the attending professional shall be notified immediately to advise the patient on the consequences. At no time however, can the staff forcibly confine or hold the patient to prevent departure.*

Cross-references: P3.4; P4.1.11; F9

(Name of Institution)

Leaving Treatment Against Advice (non-hospital)

Patient's Name: _____   _____   _____
                      (last)   (first)   (middle)

Patient Number: _____

Date: _____

Room and bed nos.: _____

Attending provider: _____

PART A

To be completed after the patient has been advised of the potential risks of leaving treatment.

I, (patient's name) _____ have decided against the advice of my attending healthcare provider, _____, to leave treatment.

I have been advised by _____ of the risks of leaving treatment, including the following:

_____

_____

_____

and have been advised not to leave.

I hereby release the healthcare provider and staff and my attending from any liability for any harm caused to me by my leaving under these circumstances.

Patient's signature: _____

Witness' signature: _____

PART B

To be completed if the patient leaves treatment before advice on leaving can be given.

(Patient's name) _____ has left treatments (check one) _____ without notifying any staff member, or _____ refusing to sign PART A of this form, and therefore was not advised of the potential risks of leaving.

The following steps have been taken to notify the patient and to advise on the risks of leaving (check as appropriate noting date and time, and individual who attempted the contact (name, department and signature):

a.   Telephone contact at numbers on records: _____   _____
                                                                       (date)   (time)

b.   E-mail contact at numbers on records: _____   _____
                                                                   (date)   (time)

c.   Telephone contacts with persons listed on
     patient record: _____   _____
                            (date)   (time)

d.   If no contact can be made, the patient shall be contacted by registered priority mail to contact the institution noting the major risks of leaving the institution: _____   _____
                                                              (date)   (time)

e.   If patient is considered a danger to himself or others, police have been advised: _____   _____
                               (date)   (time)

Items checked:

☐   Telephone contact at numbers on records:

     Name of Contact: _____

     Person making contact (print): _____

     Signature: _____

     Date/time: _____

☐   E-mail contact at numbers on records:

     Name of Contact: _____

     Person making contact (print): _____

     Signature: _____

     Date/time: _____

☐ Telephone contacts with persons listed on
patient record:

Name of Contact: _____

Person making contact (print): _____

Signature: _____

Date/time: _____

☐ If no contact can be made, the patient shall be contacted by
registered priority mail to contact the institution noting the major
risks of leaving the institution:

Name of Contact: _____

Person making contact (print): _____

Signature: _____

Date/time: _____

☐ If patient is considered a danger to himself or others, police have
been advised:

Name of Contact: _____

Person making contact (print): _____

Signature: _____

Date/time: _____

PATIENTS — Admissions/Assessments/Discharges/Exits

Form 12: Patient Representative

Objective: *The purpose of this form is to make certain that when a patient is unable to take certain actions on his or her own behalf, there is documentation that the person who takes those actions on behalf of the patient is authorized to do so.*

Application: *This form shall be reviewed by legal counsel to make certain that it conforms with provincial or territorial law. This document shall be available at all times in administrative offices and shall be administered by an administrative officer. No action shall be taken until the form has been completed.*

Cross-references: F21

(Name of Institution)
Patient Representative

I (print name) _____ of (print address) _____

_____

am representing (print name of patient) _____

of (print address) _____

_____

identified by SIN # _____

who is a patient at (name of institution) _____

I (circle one) have _____ have not _____ been appointed under the laws
of _____.
    (name of province/territory)

My relationship to the patient is as: (please circle)

a.   court-appointed guardian or trustee

b.   patient-appointed guardian or trustee

c.   parent

d.   spouse or partner by marriage

e.   child (adult only)

f.   sibling (adult only)

As a guardian or trustee of the patient I am authorized to:

_____

_____

_____

Attached is a copy of any document appointing me as guardian or trustee

Witness: (print name) _____

          (signature) _____

Date: _____

PATIENTS — Admissions/Assessments/Discharges/Exits

Form 13: Certificate of Translation

Cross-reference: P4.6

(Name of Institution)
Certificate of Translation

This is to certify that:

1.   I am knowledgeable in both the English and the _____ languages, and am able to translate spoken and written English into _____ and from _____ into English.

2.   I translated a meeting from both languages

    a.   on (date) _____,

    b.   at the _____ Hospital

    c.   with the following in attendance:

_____

3.   The notes taken at that meeting are an accurate reflection of the conversations which took place.

4.   I translated the attached documents from _____ to _____ and that these translations are an accurate translation.

Name of translator: _____

Signature of translator: _____

Date: _____

PATIENTS — Consent

Form 14: Checklist for a Valid Consent

Objective: *The purpose of this form is to ensure that all the legally required criteria for a valid informed consent have been met. Each of the criteria must be checked off, or an explanation given as to why the criteria could not be met.*

Application: *To be completed by the person who informs the patient or the patient's substitute and obtains the consent or refusal.*

Cross-references: P4.1

(Name of Institution)

Checklist for a Valid Consent

Patient's Name: _____ _____ _____
            (last)   (first)   (middle)

Date of Birth: _____

Patient Number: _____

Surgery/Treatment for which consent is being given: _____

Date of Surgery: _____

□   Consent given by the patient or a a valid substitute

□   Explanation given of the nature of the proposed procedure

□   Explanation given of the hoped-for benefits

□   Explanation given of possible risks

□   Patient or substitute informed of the right to refuse the procedure

□   Patient or substitute informed of the risks and any benefits of refusing

□   Patient or substitute mentally capable of understanding the explanation, and understanding what it means to consent

□   Patient or substitute physically capable of understanding, *i.e.*, does not have hearing problems, nor eyesight problems which would make it difficult to see any diagrams or other information

□   Neither patient nor substitute appears to be under any pressure to either consent or refuse, and has expressed desire freely

□   Patient or substitute has the linguistic ability to understand the explanation given and to communicate as part of the consent process

□   Cultural and religious values reviewed with the patient or substitute that would affect the decision to consent or refuse

□   Patient or substitute given the opportunity to ask questions and to express any concerns, doubts or disagreements

□   Patient or substitute advised that consent may be withdrawn after being given, except in circumstances in which the interruption or termination of the procedure before its completion could cause injury

Patient's Name: _____ Page (1/2)

☐   Patient is not under the influence of medication or any medical condition that would make it impossible to take part in the consent process

Person conducting the consent process: _____

Signature: _____

Date: _____

PATIENTS — Consent

Form 15: Evaluation of Patient's Capacity to Consent

Objective: *A basic criterion of a valid consent is that the patient has the mental capacity to make a decision as to whether or not to consent to a medical or surgical procedure or to refuse it. The capacity depends on the patient being able to understand that there is a legal right to consent or to refuse, and to understand the information given upon which this decision will be made. In most cases there is no question as to whether the patient has the capacity or not. However, if there is any suggestion of lack of capacity, the patient should be examined by a physician, preferably a physician other than the attending physician or a physician who may be involved in the procedure or the care of the patient. The examining physician should then complete this form so that there is evidence in the record as to the capacity, and therefore the validity of the consent or refusal.*

See Lorne E. Rozovsky, "The Canadian Law of Consent to Treatment", 3rd ed. (Markham, ON: LexisNexis Canada, 2003), pp. 10-12 and 61-78. Also see D'Arcy Hiltz and Anita Szigeti, "A Guide to Consent and Capacity Law in Ontario, 2008 Edition" (Markham, ON: LexisNexis Canada, 2007).

Application: *This form is to be used when an examination for mental capacity takes place to determine whether or not the patient has the capacity to consent or refuse treatment. If it is determined that the patient has the capacity, the process of consent or refusal of the patient may proceed. If however, the determination is that the patient lacks this capacity, consent must be sought from a substitute.*

It should be understood by the person doing the examination that the issue is related to mental capacity to take part in the consent process. It is not whether the person is mentally ill, or insane, or lacks the capacity to do other things.

It should also be noted that it is possible for the patient to have the capacity to understand the consent process related to one particular procedure, but not another.

Cross-references: P4,1

(Name of Institution)
Evaluation of Patient's Capacity to Consent

Re: Patient's Name: _____ _____ _____

                           (last)   (first)   (middle)

    Date of Birth: _____

    Patient Number: _____

I, Dr. _____ of (address) _____

_____

have examined _____, a patient in the (name of institution) on (date) _____ and have determined that the patient:

(check one) has ____ does not have ____ the mental capacity to understand the information related to the procedure of _____, which has been recommended for the patient with respect to the nature of the procedure, the risks, benefits and reasonable alternatives of undertaking the procedure or in the alternative refusing to consent to it, and the capacity to understand that there is a right either to consent or to refuse.

(signature) _____

(print name) _____

(date) _____

(witness' signature) _____

(witness' print name) _____

PATIENTS — Consent

Form 16:   Consent to Treatment

Objective: *The principle and practice of consent to treatment is initially the most important legal aspect in the commencement and provision of health care. No procedure can take place without a valid and informed consent being given apart from several notable exceptions. In an emergency in which treatment cannot be delayed without harming the patient, and the patient is not mentally capable of consenting and no substitute is available, consent is not required since it is assumed. Consent is also not required if under either communicable disease legislation or mental health legislation certain legislative criteria exist in which treatment can be given without consent and against the will of the patient. In those cases the legislative criteria must be adhered to precisely.*

The law of consent to treatment rests not on the legal right to consent, but on the legal right not to be treated. The consent consists of the patient giving up that right.

It also must be noted that what is known as the consent to treatment is not simply the form, but consists of a process by which a patient is advised of the nature, risks, benefits and reasonable alternatives of the recommended procedure, and the patient or the patient's substitute when the patient is incapable of consenting, makes a decision as to whether to consent or refuse.

The purpose of the form, which may or may not be required under provincial or territorial legislation, is primarily to provide evidence for the healthcare provider that consent has taken place, in case later litigation alleges that the procedure took place without consent, or without a valid informed consent. The problem is that the traditional form is limited in that it usually does not provide evidence of the informative part of the process, of what the patient was told. It often does not provide evidence that the patient was even mentally capable of understanding the process and that there is a right to refuse treatment.

Finally, while the phrase used is ordinarily referred to as "consent to treatment", in fact, it applies to any interference with the patient's body either directly or indirectly. It may be for diagnostic, treatment or care. It may also include treatment by medication in which medications are prescribed and taken by the patient, rather than the patient's body being "touched" by someone else.

Therefore, while this form is important, there must be an understanding as to its limitations, and that it does not operate as an excuse to begin a procedure in which a valid and informed consent has in fact taken place.

See Lorne E. Rozovsky, "The Canadian Law of Consent to Treatment", 3rd ed. (Markham, ON: LexisNexis Canada, 2003), cc. 1, 8 and 9, and Appendix II. Also D'Arcy Hiltz and Anita Szigeti, "A Guide to Consent and Capacity Law in Ontario, 2008 Edition" (Markham, ON: LexisNexis Canada, 2007).

Application: *This form is to be presented to the patient for signature, or to the person substituting for the patient, when the consent process has been completed and completed correctly.*

Cross-references: P4

| **(Name of Institution)** |
| **Consent to Treatment** |

Patient's Name: _____   _____   _____
                        (last)   (first)   (middle)

Date of Birth: _____ / _____ / _____
                        (yyyy)   (mm)   (dd)

Patient Number: _____

Attending physician: _____

Date: _____

---

1. I have been advised by Dr. _____ to undergo a (name of
    procedure) _____ in the (name of institution).

2. Dr. _____ has explained to me:

    a. The nature of the procedure, what will be done, and the care
        which I will require before, during and after the procedure.

    b. That the goal is to achieve the following benefits:

        _____ .

    c. The benefits are hoped for but cannot be guaranteed.

    d. There are the following risks of undergoing the procedure:

        _____ .

    e. There are the following reasonable alternatives to having this
        procedure done:

        _____ .

    f. There are the following risks of not undergoing the procedure:

        _____ .

3. I understand that it is my legal right to either consent to this
    procedure, or to refuse to have it done.

4. I have read the information pamphlet # _____ which has explained
    this procedure and I understand it.

5. I have had an opportunity to ask questions about the procedure, which have been answered to my satisfaction.

6. I agree that the procedure may be performed by any member of the staff of (name of institution) and may involve physicians, surgeons and other healthcare personnel, who may perform all or part of the procedure, and may be involved in my care and treatment prior to, during or after the procedure takes place.

7. I also agree to such further or alternative measures as may be found to be immediately necessary during the course of the procedure in the discretion of the attending physician in charge of the procedure.

8. I also consent to the administration of general or other anaesthetics for the purpose of carrying out the procedure.

9. I understand that the potential risks of the anaesthesia are:

_____

_____.

(signature of patient) _____

(date) _____

As I witness to the signature of this patient, it is also my belief that the patient's consent is given voluntarily without undue pressure or coercion, and that the patient is mentally capable of understanding the information given on the procedure, and that it is the legal right of the patient to decide whether to consent or refuse this procedure.

(signature of witness) _____

(print name of witness) _____

(date) _____

PATIENTS — Consent

Form 17: Refusal to Consent

Objective: *The essential legal right of a patient to consent to treatment is part of the right to refuse treatment. A consent to treatment is not valid unless the patient makes that decision based on information outlining the nature, risks, benefits and reasonable alternatives of the proposed treatment. Similarly, to make a decision not to undergo a particular procedure or a course of treatment, the patient must be advised of the risks, benefits and reasonable alternatives of refusing. The purpose of this form is to make certain that this procedure is followed in order to give the patient or a substitute for the patient, the opportunity to exercise this right. It is also designed to provide evidence for the protection of the health provider or institution that the patient has been given this opportunity, and that the refusal was made on the basis of appropriate information.*

It should be noted that the only occasion on which the patient does not have a right to refuse treatment would be in the case of a communicable disease which specifically is covered by communicable disease legislation, and in the case of forcible detention and treatment under mental health legislation if the specific criteria for compulsory treatment under that legislation have been met.

See Lorne E. Rozovsky, "The Canadian Law of Consent to Treatment", 3rd ed. (Markham, ON: LexisNexis Butterworths, 2003), c. 8 (endorsed by the Canadian Health Information Management Association).

Application: *During the consent process, when a patient or the patient's substitute is being advised of the information and recommendations upon which the consent decision will be made, the patient is to be advised that while the procedure is being recommended, he or she does have the legal right to refuse. If he or she wishes to refuse treatment, this form should be presented for signature.*

Cross-references: P4.3

(Name of Institution)
Refusal to Consent

Patient's Name: _____   _____   _____
                       (last)   (first)   (middle)

Date of Birth: _____ / _____ / _____
                          (yyyy)   (mm)   (dd)

Patient Number: _____

Attending Physician: _____

Date: _____

I, (name) _____, of (address) _____,
have been advised by Dr. _____ to undergo a procedure
identified as a _____. The nature, risks, benefits and
reasonable alternatives of this procedure have been explained to me, and I
have had an opportunity to ask questions.

I understand that I have the right to refuse any or all treatment, and hereby
refuse to consent to the recommended procedure. In making this decision I
have been informed of the risks of this decision, and agree to accept those
risks. In refusing to undergo this procedure against the recommendation of
my doctor, I agree not to hold my doctor, or the (name of institution), its
medical staff or any of its employees responsible for any consequences as
a result of my decision.

(signature) _____

(print name) _____

(signature of witness other than the doctor who advised the patient)

_____

(print name) _____

(date) _____

PATIENTS — Consent

Form 18: Telephone Consent

Objective: *Ordinarily the consent process is evidenced by a document that is signed and witnessed by the patient who has been duly informed and made the decision to proceed with the procedure. If the patient is mentally or legally incapable of consenting, the consent process is carried out with an appropriate substitute who signs the form. In some cases the patient is not mentally or legally capable of taking part in the consent process, and no substitute is physically present and is not able to be physically present or to be present within the necessary time required for the procedure to commence. This form is designed to provide some evidence that the consent process did take place with a substitute over the telephone.*

Application: *Because this form is potentially not as reliable as that which is actually signed by the substitute decision-maker in person, various questions must be asked and information received that would ordinarily not be required. Because of potential questions as to the credibility of the consent process, it is important that at least two people from the institution take part in the telephone conversation, and that this is recorded as noted in the form.*

Cross-references: P4.2; P4.4; F12; F23

| **(Name of Institution)** |
| **Telephone Consent Form** |

Patient's Name: _____   _____   _____
                      (last)   (first)   (middle)

Date of Birth: _____ / _____ / _____
                         (yyyy)   (mm)   (dd)

Patient Number: _____

Date of telephone call: _____

Time of telephone call: _____

1. Attending physician carrying out consent process: _____

2. Name of witness on telephone line: _____

3. Name of person legally authorized to act as a substitute on behalf of the patient:

        Address: _____

                 _____

        Telephone: _____

4. Relationship between the substitute and the patient (add details):

    _____

    _____

5. Efforts made to ensure the accuracy of the substitute's authority:

    _____

    _____

6. Telephone number at which substitute was reached: _____

7. Reason for substitute being asked to consent:

    a. patient not mentally capable of consenting: Yes ___ No ___

    b. patient not legally capable of consenting: Yes ___ No ___

    c. delay in obtaining consent by patient or with substitute present could cause injury: Yes ___ No ___

    d. substitute unable to be present prior to necessity of procedure taking place: Yes ___ No ____

Patient's Name: _____ Page (1/2)

The following information shall be conveyed to the substitute decision-maker (check off confirming that this was done):

☐   name and position of person calling and name and position of person acting as a witness

☐   purpose of call and necessity of having a substitute

☐   role of substitute decision-making and that there is no financial obligation involved

☐   information requested on substitute's relationship to patient

NOTE: If the substitute is not a parent, spouse, adult child, or adult sibling, or legally appointed as guardian of the patient, consent cannot be given by the substitute, and the matter is to be referred to the CEO and legal counsel.

☐   all information which would ordinarily be required in any consent process, *i.e.*, nature, risks, benefits of procedure, and any reasonable alternatives, as well as risks of not undergoing the procedure

☐   opportunity for questions

☐   request for follow-up signed consent form

☐   contact information for substitute with the healthcare providing institution

☐   offer to provide updated progress information on the progress of the patient

Calling Physician (signature and name in print): _____

Witness (signature and name in print): _____

Date: _____   _____

PATIENTS — Consent

Form 19: Emergencies without Consent

Objective: *The purpose of this form is to provide evidence that an emergency existed in such circumstances so as to provide a legal exception to the rule that no procedure can take place without consent.*

Application: *This form is to be completed by the attending physician having determined that each of the criteria for an emergency exception to the consent requirement has been met, and that the procedure can take place without consent.*

Cross-references: P4.5

(Name of Institution)
Emergencies Without Consent

Patient's Name: _____   _____   _____
　　　　　　　　　　(last)　　　　　　(first)　　　　　(middle)

Date of Birth: _____ / _____ / _____
　　　　　　　　　　(yyyy)　　　　　　(mm)　　　　　(dd)

OHIP: _____

SIN: _____

Patient Number: _____

Date: _____　Time: _____

I, _____, the attending physician of (patient)_____ certify that:

a.　the patient is not mentally capable of understanding the information required to give a valid and informed consent for the following procedures: _____

_____ ;

b.　that a delay in performing the procedure until the patient is mentally capable of consenting is likely to cause serious injury or cause a risk of death to the patient;

c.　that there is no person who has to authority to give consent on the patient's behalf prior to the necessity of the procedure being performed;

d.　that the procedure is required for the health or life of the patient; and

e.　that the procedure be performed as quickly as possible without consent.

Signature of physician: _____ _____

Printed name of physician: _____

Signature of witness: _____

Printed name of witness: _____

Date: _____

Time: _____

PATIENTS — Consent

Form 20: Consent of Children (Minors)

Objective: *The purpose of this form is to provide evidence that the patient who is under the age of majority, that is a minor, is mentally capable of consenting to treatment, unless provincial or territorial legislation specifically prohibits the patient from consent on his or her own behalf.*

Application: *This form is to be completed by a physician, who preferably is not the physician who is to treat the patient. Once a determination has been made that the patient is mentally capable of consenting to treatment, until provincial or territorial legislation states otherwise, the patient is legally capable of consenting on his or her own behalf, and no one else has the authority to give a substitute consent, unless there is a mental incapacity in which case, a substitute will have the authority to consent.*

Cross-references: P4.4; F20; F21; F23

(Name of Institution)

Consent of Children (Minors)

Patient's Name: _____   _____   _____
                   (last)   (first)   (middle)

Date of Birth: _____ / _____ / _____
                   (yyyy)   (mm)   (dd)

OHIP: _____

Patient Number: _____

Address: _____

Telephone: _____

Attending physician: _____

Institution: _____

I, _____, a duly licensed physician in the Province
(or Territory) of _____ having examined _____,

certify that the patient has the mental capacity to understand the information
given upon which the patient will base a decision as to whether to undergo the
procedure of _____ as proposed by _____,
the attending physician.

The patient understands the nature, risks and benefits of undergoing the
procedure, and the risks and potential benefits of not undergoing the
procedure, and understands that there is no compulsion to undergo the
procedure.

_____

Name of physician examining for the purpose of this form: _____

Signature of physician: _____

Name of attending physician: _____

Signature of attending physician: _____

Date: _____

Hours: _____

PATIENTS — Consent

Form 21: Authorization for Substitute Consent for a Child

Objective: *The purpose of this form is to allow healthcare providers to provide care and treatment to children who clearly do not have the mental capability of consenting on their own behalf and whose parents or guardians are not available.*

Application: *Ordinarily if a child is brought to a healthcare institution for treatment by someone who is not a parent or guardian such as a childcare worker, babysitter, teacher or relative, the consent of the parent or guardian must be obtained. If, however, an emergency exists in which the care cannot be delayed without jeopardizing the life or health of the child, care that is restricted to alleviating that emergency can be given without consent being given.*

Cross-references: P4.4; F12; F18; F19

(Name of Institution)
Authorization for Substitute Consent for a Child

Re: (Patient's Name): _____   _____   _____
         (last)   (first)   (middle)

Date of Birth: _____ / _____ / _____
      (yyyy)   (mm)   (dd)

OHIP: _____

Patient Number: _____

Address: _____

We, _____ and _____ of (address) _____, _____ in the Province /Territory of _____, being the parents or legally appointed foster parents of the minor _____ and having the lawful custody of the said minor, hereby authorize _____ of (address) _____

in the Province/Territory of _____, to consent to any medically necessary care, treatment or diagnostic procedures by any physician, surgeon, or dentist or any employee or staff member of any hospital, clinic or diagnostic centre during our absence from the said _____ of _____ or when we are otherwise unable to give our consent to such care, treatment or procedures.

Signature: _____

Print name: _____

Relationship to child: _____

Signature: _____

Print name: _____

Relationship to child: _____

Date: _____

Address: _____

PATIENTS — Consent

Form 22: Advance Directive

Objective: *The purpose of this form is to notify all interested parties, both healthcare providers and family, in order to avoid disputes over what a patient would or would not have wanted. It is also evidence of refusal to consent to particular procedures that might ordinarily be undertaken in case of an emergency when the patient is unable to consent. As a result of this form, these procedures would be prohibited. Adapted from "The Canadian Law of Consent to Treatment", 3rd ed., by Lorne E. Rozovsky (Markham, ON: LexisNexis Butterworths, 2003), Appendix 4.*

Application: *All members of the public should be encouraged to have an advance directive in order to avoid disputes and unwanted care and procedures should a catastrophic illness take place when the patient is not capable of making personal treatment and care decisions. However, it is vitally important that those who may be involved or have a direct interest in the care of the patient be aware that an advance directive exists and have a copy of it. Physicians should be encouraged to provide copies to their patients, and to file a copy with the physician. Similarly, spouses and children should also have copies. In cases of serious illness, hospital and long-term care patients should also be encouraged to complete an advance directive.*

If at any time a change is made in the advance directive, any person who has a copy should be notified of the change, be given a revised copy and be advised to destroy the previous copy.

Every person who is given a copy should be aware of the others who have also been given copies. Each person who has a copy should keep it in a place where it is immediately accessible, such as a dresser drawer, and not a bank deposit vault.

This form should be reviewed by legal counsel to ensure that it conforms with any provincial or territorial law.

Cross-references: P4.3; F17; F22

ADVANCE DIRECTIVE OF (name)

effective on and after (date)

I, _____ of the City of _____, in the Province/Territory of _____, the County of _____, declare as follows:

1. If at any time I should suffer from a condition in which I am not capable of understanding or not capable of giving directions to my physician with respect to my care or treatment; and

   a. my condition has been determined by two physicians as being irreversible or incurable; or

   b. my condition has been determined by two physicians as being terminal,

I hereby direct as follows:

   a. I am not to be given extraordinary treatment that would maintain or continue my life, including, but not restricted to, life support systems, nasal gastric feeding, antibiotics, cardiopulmonary resuscitation, ventilation or surgery; and

   b. any treatment or care, including, but not restricted to, life support systems, nasal gastric feeding, antibiotics and ventilation that may be maintaining my life artificially shall be withdrawn.

2. It is my desire that this directive be honoured by my family, physicians and all those concerned with my care as a final expression of my legal right to refuse medical or surgical treatment or care.

3. I understand and accept the potential consequences of this direction including that of death.

4. This directive shall remain in effect until it may be revoked by me.

Made on the ___ day of ____ 200__

Signature: _____

Advance Directive of: _____ Page (1/2)

As witnesses to this document, we:

  a.   are personally acquainted with the declarant;

  b.   are witnessing this document at the request of the declarant, who is an adult;

  c.   believe the declarant to be of sound mind and to have a full understanding of the action being taken in this declaration and the possible consequences of it;

  d.   are not related to the declarant by blood or marriage;

  e.   are not entitled to any portion of the estate of the declarant on the death of the declarant, under any will or by law, nor do we have any claim against the estate of the declarant; and

  f.   are not physicians or health professionals attending to the declarant, nor employees of any attending healthcare provider of the declarant nor of any institution in which the declarant is currently a patient or a resident.

Sworn to at _____ ,   Witness (signature): _____

In the County of _____ ,   Print name: _____

Province/Territory of _____ ,   Witness (signature): _____

This day of _____ , 200_   Print name: _____

Before

(notary public)

Copies given to: a. _____

                    b. _____

                    c. _____

PATIENTS — Consent

Form 23: Letter to Jehovah's Witness Parents

Objective: *The purpose of this form is to advise parents who would have the authority to consent to treatment over a child as to the potential risks of refusing to consent to blood transfusions or other procedures involving blood products. It fulfills the same requirement that an adult has in having the right to be advised of the risks of not consenting to any treatment that is being recommended. In this case, because the situation involves a child who does not have the capability of consenting or refusing, the parents have the same rights of being advised over treatment regarding the child as an adult would. The exception, however, is that society by law has the authority to override the parents' refusal in certain circumstances, and the healthcare provider may have the legal obligation to notify public authorities.*

The second purpose of the form is not only to meet the legal rights of the parents to be informed, but to have evidence in a potential defence that this information has been provided.

Application: *It is important that this document be prepared as soon as there is an indication the Jehovah's Witness parents intend to refuse treatment for their child. Generally speaking, parents are prepared to sign waivers of liability in these cases, though it is important that this notification be given. If it is found that the parents disagree, either because one is not a Jehovah's Witness, or there has been a divorce or separation, the matter should immediately be referred to the risk manager and legal counsel of the hospital.*

It is also important that the receipt of the letter be acknowledged either by witness if it is delivered personally, or by registered mail.

Cross-references: P4.4

(Name of Institution)

Letter to Jehovah's Witness Parents

Re: For the care of (patient's name): _____   _____   _____
         (last)   (first)   (middle)

Date of Birth: _____ / _____ / _____
                    (yyyy)   (mm)   (dd)

Patient Number: _____

The _____ Hospital and its staff understand that the parents or substitute decision-makers of children who are of the Jehovah's Witness faith usually do not want their children to be given blood or blood products.

As a result, the medical staff will attempt to find means of treating the child with alternate means that do not conflict with the Jehovah's Witness beliefs.

If, however, the attending physician of the child believes that there is no viable alternative and that blood or blood products must be given against the wishes of the parents or substitute decision-makers of the child, the physician may call the Children's Aid Society or other appropriate authority to obtain permission for such treatment.

If such action is taken, you will be notified immediately.

In case of a life-threatening emergency however, medical staff will provide whatever treatment is permitted by law. This may include the administration of blood or blood products.

(signature of attending physician) _____

(print name) _____

(date) _____

_____   _____

A signed copy of this letter is to be placed in the front of the patient's record and is to be updated if the child is moved to another unit

I (we) have read and understood this letter.

This is not my (our) agreement for the administration of blood or blood products for our child, nor do I (we) give up any of my (our) legal rights regarding the consent to the medical or surgical care of my (our) child.

(signature of parent(s) or guardian(s)) _____

(print name(s) and relationship to child) _____

(date) _____

(address) _____

PATIENTS — Consent

Form 24: Consent to Telehealth

Objective: *Telehealth involves the transmission of information regarding the patient's condition including the direct transmission of diagnostic results for the advice and consultation of experts who are geographically distant from where the patient is being treated. The information is sent electronically to a location either in the same locale, or elsewhere within the country, or anywhere in the world. The purpose is to be able to receive advice from an individual or a centre that has the expertise not available in the patient's location, and to have access to the best advice available in the world regardless of distance.*

The result is that the patient's information is not restricted to the patient's own doctors or hospital. It is this aspect that may be of some concern and for that reason the patient should be advised of this aspect and asked for consent.

The second issue arising from telehealth is that the person being consulted does not have privileges in the hospital in which the patient is being treated, and therefore does not have the responsibilities or involvement that a regular member of the medical staff has. The patient should be advised of this, and of the procedures that are undertaken in order to maintain quality.

Application: *If the resources of the telehealth system are to be used, the patient should be advised and asked to consent. This form is then used as evidence that this has taken place.*

Cross-references: P4.1

(Name of Institution)

Consent to Telehealth

Patient's Name: _____   _____   _____
                        (last)   (first)   (middle)

Date of Birth: _____ / _____ / _____
                        (yyyy)   (mm)   (dd)

Substitute for patient (if applicable): _____

Patient Number: _____

Date: _____

Attending physician: _____

Dear Patient:

During the course of your care at this institution, advantage will be taken of professional advice available not only within our institution and community but elsewhere in the world. This will be done by the Telehealth system in which information gathered by your doctors or by the various diagnostic procedures conducted here will be sent electronically to consultants and experts elsewhere. While the information gathered will be sent electronically to the consultants, it will be sent under an identifying number and not under your name or any number ordinarily associated with you. Your privacy will therefore be assured.

The consultants to whom the information will be sent for advice are not members of the medical staff of this institution, but whose credentials have been reviewed by this institution to determine that they meet or exceed the standards required of this institution, and can provide you and your doctor with advice and expertise that would otherwise not be available. Your own doctor, however, will remain in charge of your care and treatment.

(Signature of patient): _____

Witness (signature & printed name): _____

Date: _____

PATIENTS — Consent

Form 25: Consent to be Photographed

Objective: *In many situations it may be questionable as to whether the patient has a legal right not to be photographed while under care or treatment. It may in some situations even be assumed that in consenting to the procedure the consent to be photographed is implied. In order to avoid such a misunderstanding from arising which could result not only in legal or threatened legal proceedings, or at least damage the relationship between the patient and the health institution or healthcare provider, it is preferable to openly advise the patient that photography may be used, and that the consent of the patient is requested. However, once this is done, it then becomes very important not to go against any refusal which can certainly cause the very problems that one is attempting to avoid. This form is based on a form in Lorne E. Rozovsky and Noela J. Inions, "Canadian Health Information: A Practical Legal and Risk Management Guide", 3rd ed. (Markham, ON: Butterworths Canada, 2002), p. 224.*

Application: *This form should be given to the patient as part of the admission process or prior to a situation in which photography is anticipated. In some cases, photography may be necessary to assist in the treatment process, such as in facial plastic surgery.*

Cross-references: P4.1

(Name of Institution)
Consent to be Photographed

To (name of institution):

I, _____, give my consent for the taking of photographs of _____ (area of body to be photographed) by _____ (name of photographer or name of institution). I understand that these photographs will be used by the _____ (name of health facility) for the purpose of study or medical research, or to assist in the care, treatment or diagnosis of my condition, and that no information which might reveal my personal identity shall be revealed to anyone other than those who are directly responsible or involved with my care.

I also understand that these photographs will not be reprinted, published or otherwise reproduced in any scientific or academic journal or book or any other publication, or other means of reproduction, without my further written authorization. This includes transmission by any electronic means to any permission except a person who is directly involved with my care.

(patient's name) _____

(patient's signature) _____

(witness' signature) _____

(witness' printed name) _____

(date) _____

PATIENTS — Diagnoses/Treatments

Form 26: Reports to be Received

Objective: *The purpose of this form is to prevent situations in which diagnosis or treatment might be delayed or not done at all because a report or a consult which was requested has not been received. To effectively use this form, the file must be re-activated and action taken whether or not a report has been received.*

Application: *This form is to be used by the healthcare provider (physician, dentist, etc.) in conjunction with the administrative personnel responsible for managing the practice of the healthcare provider.*

Use of form:

- *Place this form on the exterior of the patient's file.*

- *List items such as consults, lab tests, appointments, etc. The file is to be recorded in a daily diary under the date on which the report should be received. This date is to be chosen by experience as to how long it usually takes to obtain a reply. The file is to be pulled on the date when the report should have been received.*

- *If the report is not received by that date, the matter is to be followed up by letter, e-mail or telephone call with the date noted, a copy of the follow-up or a note to be placed in the file, and a date noted when a reply can be expected from the follow-up.*

- *If it is urgent that the report be received the file must be referred to the responsible physician to take whatever action may be necessary.*

Cross-references: P5.1; F3; F5; F6; F7; F27; F28

(Name of Institution)						
Reports to be Received						

Patient's Name: _____   _____ _____
                         (last)   (first)   (middle)

Date of Birth: _____ / _____ / _____
                          (yyyy)   (mm)   (dd)

Patient Number: _____

	Reports expected	Date expected	Received Y	Received N	Follow-up	Initials
1						
2						
3						
4						
5						
6						
7						

PATIENTS — DIAGNOSES/TREATMENTS

Form 27:   External Diagnostic Tests

Objective: *This form is used as a record to be filed under the date on which the results are expected. If when the form is pulled and the results have not arrived, follow-up action is taken and the form is to be refiled under a subsequent date when results are again expected. The purpose of this form is the same as Form 26 (Reports to be Received). It is to ensure that reports that are expected are in fact received so that diagnosis or treatment is not delayed and does take place. The copy of any documentation that went with the sample is to be filed in the patient's record.*

Application: *This form is to used by the person who manages the practice, and who is responsible for the timely and accurate diagnostic and treatment services.*

Cross-references: P5.1; F3; F5; F6; F7; F26; F28; F29; F30

(Name of Institution)	
External Diagnostic Tests	

(Check one) □ **URGENT** □ **NON-URGENT**

Patient's Name: _____ _____ _____
                    (last)   (first)   (middle)

Date of Birth: _____ / _____ / _____
                    (yyyy)   (mm)   (dd)

OHIP: _____

Patient Number: _____

Referring physician: _____

Test requested:	_____ _____ Check one: □ **Sample sent to:** _____ □ **Sample or test (*e.g.*, x-ray) done at:** _____ _____ **Date results expected:** _____ **Received:** □ **yes** □ **no**
	1. Results not received, action taken (check and date): **Telephone call made:** _____ **Letter:** _____ **Patient notified for repeat sample:** _____ **Date results expected:** _____ **Received:** □ **yes** □ **no**

Patient's Name: _____ Page (1/2)

	2. Results received, action taken (check and date):
	□ **Results given to referring physician**
	□ **Patient notified by telephone**
	□ **Patient notified by mail**
	□ **Follow-up appointment made**
	□ **Patient referred elsewhere (note where)**

PATIENTS — Diagnoses/Treatments

Form 28: Request for Consultation Checklist

Objective: *The purpose of this form is to enhance correct and timely communication between the referring physician (or other healthcare provider) and the consultant, so that the patient will receive the appropriate treatment in a timely manner.*

Application: *This checklist is to be used when a letter requesting a consultant's opinion is being sent. Its purpose is to ensure that the information needed by the consultant is included and that the information is correct. It is also useful to make certain that the letter contains a very specific request so that the consultant will provide the information or the opinions required by the referring physician.*

The letter of consultation is to be filed in the patient's record along with Forms 6 and 29, which are filed separately to track that a reply has been received. When the reply is received, a review of the letter should be made to make certain that all of the information or opinions requested were provided. Action taken on the basis of missing or incorrect information resulting in patient injury may be considered as medical negligence, if the physician or other care provider knew or ought to have known that the information given by the consultant was missing or incorrect, or based on information that was missing or incorrect.

In the letter requesting the consultation, it is important to number each item so that the consultant may respond to each in turn.

A note should also be made as to whether the patient was to make any arrangements and whether the patient was informed of this fact. If no arrangements for a consultation were made and the patient was relying on the physician's office, this may also result in patient injury and a possible allegation of negligence.

Cross-references: P5.1; F3; F5; F6; F7; F26; F29; F30

(Name of Institution)
Request for Consultation Checklist

Patient's Name: _____   _____   _____
            (last)   (first)   (middle)

Date of Birth: _____ / _____ / _____
                    (yyyy)   (mm)   (dd)

OHIP: _____

Patient Number: _____

Referring physician: _____

Consultation requested of: _____

_____

Date of request for consultation: _____

Appointment made with consultant (if necessary): ☐ yes   ☐ no

☐ By patient   ☐ by referring physician

• When made _____

• Date of appointment _____

Letter requesting consultation contains (check each one):

☐ purpose of request

☐ medical history

☐ issues to be addressed (number each in separate paragraphs)

☐ statement regarding whether urgent and date on which it is required

Follow-up:

☐   appointment made with referring physician (date) _____

☐   patient advised of consultation request (date) _____

☐   reply received from consultant

☐   action taken:

_____

_____

PATIENTS — Diagnoses/Treatments

Form 29: External Consultation

Objective: *This form is used as a record to be filed under the date on which a reply to a request for an external consultant's opinion is expected. The form is to be pulled on that date. If a reply has not been received, follow-up action is to be taken and the form is to be refiled under a subsequent date when results are again expected. A copy of the letter or other documentation requesting the consultation is to be filed in the patient's record. The purpose therefore is similar to that of Form 26. It is to ensure that the reports which are expected are in fact received so that diagnosis or treatment is not delayed and does take place.*

Application: *This form is to be used by the person who manages the practice, and who is responsible for the timely and accurate diagnostic and treatment services.*

Cross-references: P5.1; F3; F5; F6; F7; F26; F27; F28; F29; F30

(Name of Institution)		
External Consultation		
(Check one) □ **URGENT** □ **NON-URGENT**		

Patient's Name: _____ _____ _____
(last)   (first)   (middle)

Date of Birth: _____ / _____ / _____
(yyyy)   (mm)   (dd)

Patient Number: _____

Referring physician: _____

Consultation requested of:	_____ _____ Check one: □ **Sample sent to:** _____ □ **Sample or test (*e.g.*, x-ray) done at:** _____ _____ **Date results expected:** _____ **Received:** □ **yes** □ **no**
	1. Results not received, action taken (check and date): **Telephone call made:** _____ **Letter:** _____ **Patient notified for repeat sample:** _____ **Date results expected:** _____ **Received:** □ **yes** □ **no**

Patient's Name: _____ Page (1/2)

2. Results received, action taken (check and date):

☐ **Results given to referring physician**

☐ **Patient notified by telephone**

☐ **Patient notified by mail**

☐ **Follow-up appointment made**

☐ **Patient referred elsewhere (note where)**

PATIENTS — Diagnoses/Treatments

Form 30: Medication Record

Objective: *This form is designed to assist in the accuracy of communicating information regarding drugs, and to assist in avoiding errors.*

One of the most common risks in providing healthcare is that of medication errors. These errors may occur in the prescribing of an incorrect drug or an incorrect dosage of a drug, the communicating of the prescription, the dispensing of the drug and the administration of it. Errors may result in patient injury or ineffective treatment, both of which may raise the possibility of an allegation of negligence.

Included in the form is a printed list of the 10 most common drugs used by the physician in particular cases, so that legibility will not be in question.

Application: *The form is to be used by healthcare providers who either prescribe drugs for a patient or order non-prescription drugs. It includes both prescription and non-prescription drugs, including samples given to the patients, prescriptions telephoned to a pharmacist, and advice for non-prescription drugs given to the patient over the telephone or in person.*

Any changes in dosages or frequency should constitute a new entry. Do not cross out or make changes in existing entries.

Complications/remarks should contain any special instructions to the patient and any potential drug or food interactions.

Cross-references: P5.1

(Name of Institution)
Current Medications
* This form MUST always be kept up to date. Any additions, deletions or alterations are to be noted as soon as they occur.

Patient's Name: _____   _____   _____
                        (last)   (first)   (middle)

Date of Birth: _____ / _____ / _____
                          (yyyy)   (mm)   (dd)

Patient Number: _____

Name	dosage	frequency	date begun	date ended	complications/ remarks

PATIENTS — Diagnoses/Treatments

Form 31: Unexpected Outcome

Objective: *This form is designed to assist the risk management operations of the institution in containing the risk of liability proceedings, and to develop policies and procedures to lessen unexpected outcomes in the future.*

Application: *This form is to be completed by the risk manager in order to ensure that unexpected outcomes are handled by staff in a compassionate, caring manner so that both the interests of the patient and the institution are protected.*

Cross-references: P5.1

(Name of Institution)		
Unexpected Outcome		
* This form is to be completed by the risk manager		
Patient's Name:	_____ _____ _____ (last) (first) (middle)		
Date of Birth:	_____ / _____ / _____ (yyyy) (mm) (dd)		
Patient Number:	_____		
Date of occurrence:	_____ / _____ / _____ (yyyy) (mm) (dd)		
Reported by:	_____		
Attending physician:	_____		
Details of outcome:	_____		
Location:	_____		
Attending physician:	_____		
Others in attendance:	_____		
Action of staff:	_____ _____		
Reported to department head:	□ yes □ no		

Discussion with: (check each as completed). Notes are to be made of each discussion.

- Patient (date): _____ / _____ / _____
                  (yyyy)   (mm)   (dd)

- Department head (date): _____ / _____ / _____
                                (yyyy)   (mm)   (dd)

- Attending physician (date): _____ / _____ / _____
                                        (yyyy)   (mm)   (dd)

- CEO (date): _____ / _____ / _____
                  (yyyy)   (mm)   (dd)

- Legal counsel (date): _____ / _____ / _____
                            (yyyy)   (mm)   (dd)

Report to legal counsel	(date) _____

PATIENTS — Patient's Information

Form 32: Notice of Possible Loss or Theft of Patient Information

Objective: *Because of the risks associated with identity theft, healthcare providers and institutions and others with access to patient information have a duty to protect the confidentiality of patient information. This includes any information that could conceivably identify patients or their substitutes such as social insurance numbers, medicare numbers, names, telephone numbers, addresses, e-mail addresses, employment information, welfare information, diagnoses, etc. In the event that any of this information goes missing or is stolen, the provider must act reasonably to control the risk of harm to the patient. This applies regardless of whether it is stored electronically, including any audio or visual records, or in paper format.*

The purpose of this form is to set in place a system which alerts the patient to this potentiality, since the earlier steps are taken, the more likely damage can be avoided or at least lessened. It places a certain amount of responsibility on the patient or someone acting for the patient to take action. It also provides the institution with evidence that it has acted responsibly and reasonably under the circumstances once it becomes aware of the potential risk.

Application: *As soon as the institution or provider becomes aware that personal information of patients is missing, it is vital that immediate action be taken. The institution must bring in the police immediately, and notify medical and health authorities. It should also set up a toll-free long distance number with someone who is knowledgeable in the issue, and based on the advice of legal counsel and other authorities, can appropriately advise patients.*

Notification should also be given by this form, to all patients who are or may be identified in the missing information. Notification should be given by mail. Because it may not be possible to reach all patients, advertisements in the local press, a press release to the coverage area of the public media and a notice on the institution's web site should be made.

Personal details in these announcements should not be used. Instead the notice should be in the form of a request for all patients who have received services during the affected time period to contact the institution or provider.

Cross-references: P5.5

(Name of Institution)

Notice of Possible Loss or Theft of Patient Information

URGENT !

NOTICE TO ALL PATIENTS OF (name of institution) _____

WHO RECEIVED SERVICES BETWEEN (date) _____

AND (date) _____.

From: _____

     Executive Director

     (name of institution) _____

It has come to our attention that during the period of _____ to _____ information relating to many of our patients has gone missing. At this point, we do not know if the information has been stolen, or lost through a systems error, or by some other means. There may be no reason to be concerned, but as this is confidential information, we are taking every means possible to track the cause and to lessen any injury or damage or inconvenience which could result.

We are working closely with the appropriate law enforcement officials, our own security personnel, and provincial medicare and health authorities.

One of our main concerns is the possibility of identity theft, in which through the personal identifiers, it may be possible for persons either in Canada or elsewhere in the world, to commit fraud and theft under the guise of your identity.

We are therefore, asking for your assistance.

Immediately call the hospital at 1-800------- to determine whether you are affected by this incident, and what action you should be taking. Again we apologize for this incident, which gives us a great deal of concern, and thank you for helping us in overcoming it.

(date of notice) _____

PATIENTS — Patient's Information

Form 33: Notice of Lost or Incorrect Patient Test Results

Objective: *The purpose of this form is to quickly advise the patient that test results have either been lost or for some reason appear to be incorrect, and that the test has to be repeated. The healthcare provider who ordered the test or the institution which was to receive the test is under an obligation to the patient to take all reasonable steps to ensure that test results are correct, since a diagnosis or continued care may depend on the results.*

Application: *If results from a test taken by the patient have not been received and subsequent follow-up reveals that the results have been lost, or if in reviewing the results it is obvious that they are incorrect, and it is determined that the tests should be repeated, this form letter should be sent to the patient with a follow-up telephone call.*

Cross-references: P5.5; F26

(Name of Institution)

Notice of Lost or Incorrect Patient Test Results

Dear Patient:

It has come to our attention that (check one):

☐   the results of your _____ taken on (date) _____, have never been received and apparently have been lost, we can only assume in transit.

☐   in reviewing the results of your _____ taken on (date) _____, it appears that the results may be incorrect.

Because these results are important in determining a correct diagnosis or for your continuing care and treatment, we would appreciate your calling our office to reschedule the repetition of these tests. We apologize for this inconvenience, but it is important that the quality of your care be maintained.

(signature) _____

(print name) _____

(position) _____

(name of institution or office) _____

(date) _____

PATIENTS — Patient's Information

Form 34: Researcher's Pledge of Confidentiality

Objective: *While much medical research in Canada is under the "Tri-Council Policy Statement: Ethical Conduct for Research Involving Humans", it is important that the institution in which the research takes place has a direct contractual link with researchers concerning matters of confidentiality. The purpose of this form is to accomplish this and to enable the institution to enforce the confidentiality and to give it a clear obligation to do so.*

Application: *A procedure must be established that will enable the board of the institution to consider what research takes place on its premises, who is responsible for it, and that all necessary supervision and control over the research takes place. This not only protects the interests and rights of the patients who may be research subjects but protects the instiution from liability for actions of which it knew or ought to have known that did not meet appropriate research standards. This form deals with one aspect of that procedure, namely that of confidentiality. See Lorne E. Rozovsky and Noela J. Inions, "Canadian Health Information: A Practical Legal and Risk Management Guide", 3rd ed. (Markham, ON: Butterworths Canada, 2002), c. 16.*

Cross-references: P5.5.5

(Name of Institution)
Researcher's Pledge of Confidentiality

I understand that as a researcher working in the (name of institution) I shall maintain strict confidentiality of information involving the use of research subjects' records and any information, including the identity of subjects.

I agree not to disclose or discuss such information without the consent of the subjects involved and the authorization of the appropriate authority of the (name of institution).

I understand that my research at the institution takes place solely at the discretion of the institution, and that the failure to abide by this pledge may result in my removal from the institution. I also agree that I am solely responsible for any failure to abide by this pledge, and that in the event of litigation for unauthorized disclosure of information, I agree to indemnify the institution for any damages incurred including legal costs.

(researcher's signature) _____

(researcher's name in print) _____

(witness's signature) _____

(witness's name in print) _____

(date) _____

PATIENTS — Removal of Human Remains

Form 35: Removal of Human Remains

Objective: *The purpose of this form is to ensure that human remains or parts are appropriately disposed of according to law and the wishes of the deceased or patient, or such person who has legal authority to direct the disposition. The disposition of human remains frequently arouses deep emotional responses and conflicts. Every effort must be taken to avoid such instances and that those involved be dealt with in a compassionate and understanding manner within any legal restraints that may exist. Failure to handle these matters appropriately may result in unnecessary litigation, disciplinary complaints and complaints to government and the press.*

Application: *This form is to be used with appropriate changes for the removal of human remains including fetuses, and amputated limbs. It is important that the form be immediately accessible to those administrative personnel who must authorize the disposition. It must be very clear that no member of staff is authorized to arrange for or authorize disposition without appropriate administrative approval following review of this document. Note that if this is a medical examiner's case, that part of the form must be completed. It is important to ensure that there is evidence of the proper authorization of the removal of the remains, and that the remains were delivered and received by someone who is authorized to receive them.*

Cross-references: P5.1

(Name of Institution)
Removal of Human Remains

Patient's Name: _____   _____   _____
                       (last)   (first)   (middle)

Date of Birth: _____ / _____ / _____
                          (yyyy)   (mm)   (dd)

OHIP: _____

SIN: _____

Patient Number: _____

Date of death and time: _____ / _____ / _____   _____: _____
                                    (yyyy)   (mm)   (dd)

Medical examiner's case: □ yes   □ no

A. This Part is to be completed if the death is not a medical examiner's case

1. I, _____hereby authorize the removal of (check one):

□   the remains of (name of deceased) _____

□   the remains of the foetus of (name of mother) _____

□   the stillborn remains of the (male) ___ (female) _____ born to

_____ (mother) on _____ (date)

□   the amputated limbs or other body parts of _____

2. I have the authority to issue this authorization in my position as

_____

(guardian of deceased patient, parent of minor patient unable of consent, mother of foetus or stillborn).

3. The remains specified in this authorization are to be transferred to (name and address of funeral home, crematorium or medical school)

_____

Person authorizing removal and disposition:

(name) (signature) _____

(print name) _____

(address) _____

(telephone) _____

Identification and evidence of authorization confirmed by:

(name) _____

(institutional affiliation) _____

(address) _____

(telephone) _____

The remains authorized for removal were received by

(name of institution, *e.g.*, funeral home, medical school, *etc.*):

(signature of representative) _____

(print name of representative) _____

(date) _____   (time) _____

B. If medical examiner's case (copy of authorizing document attached):

a.   call made to medical examiner's office by (print and initial)

b.   date and time of call:

c.   remains removed from within institution (location):

d.   date and time:

c.   removal by (name of staff member and ID number):

f.   acceptance by medical examiner's office official.

       Print name:

       Signature:

(date) _____   (time) _____

g.   Identification and authorization confirmed by (institution staff member):

Print name (and ID number): _____

Signature: _____

PATIENTS — Patient's Complaints

Form 36: Patient's Complaints

Objective: *The purpose of this form is to make certain that when a patient has a complaint, that there is evidence of that complaint, that it accurately reflects the complaint, provides sufficient and appropriate information on which to investigate, and records that action was taken. The first goal is to deal specifically with the particular complaint so that it does not become a matter for possible litigation or other more serious proceedings. The second is to provide information of all complaints over regular time periods in order to analyze the source and causes of complaints so that action may be taken to lessen the cause of these complaints through administrative or policy action.*

Application: *Complaints from patients must not only be welcomed but also be encouraged, since it is to the advantage of the healthcare provider and the institution to know about these complaints early in order to respond to them. Patients and their families must be assured that complaints are encouraged and that the care and service expected is not jeopardized by a complaint. Forms should be available to patients without them having to make a request. It is also important that the complaint can be sealed, and given to the patient representative or risk manager since patients may be uncomfortable in giving it to the person about whom they have a complaint.*

It must be remembered that once the complaint has been received reasonable action in response must be taken and recorded. Failure to do this may be evidence itself of negligence in not responding to a situation that could conceivably cause patient injury.

It is also important that administrative personnel personally visit the patient to at least assure the patient that the complaint has been received and is being acted on. Failure to do this can easily cause frustration and resentment, which may escalate into more serious action.

Cross-references: P7.2

(Name of Institution)

Patient's Complaint Form

TO OUR PATIENTS: In our efforts to achieve a standard of care and service, we rely very much on the involvement and opinions of our patients and their families. Occasionally, we may not have met your expectations and want to do better. One of the best ways we can achieve this is by hearing from you. If you or your families find anything that could have been better in your care and service, please complete this form and let us know. We shall do everything we can to correct the situation and improve. At no time, will your care or treatment be harmed by the fact that you have completed this form.

When you complete the form, fold it and seal it, and call the patient representative (telephone ext. _____) who will come to collect it. Thank you very much for your assistance in helping make this hospital everything that we all want it to be.

Re (name of patient representative): _____

Name of Patient:_____   _____   _____
                      (last)   (first)   (middle)

Patient Number: _____

Date of incident or time period: _____

Description of incident or incidents: _____

_____

_____

_____

Were complaints made orally?   □ Yes   □ No

To whom (either by name or position): _____

Was any action taken?   □ Yes   □ No

What action was taken? _____

_____

_____

Did a similar incident occur again?   □ Yes   □ No

Patient's Complaint Form: _____ Page (1/2)

When? (date) _____

      (time) _____

FOR OFFICE USE ONLY

Date received: _____

Personal response to patient or family: _____

_____

Referred to (check as necessary):

    ☐ executive director   ☐ medical director   ☐ risk manager

    ☐ director of nursing   ☐ director of dietary   ☐ legal counsel

Follow-up action: _____

_____

_____

Further action required:

_____

_____

Recorded for overall study and analysis (check when done): ☐

Subsequent monitoring details:

_____

_____

GENERAL STAFF AND OFFICE
ADMINISTRATION — Medical Staff Privileges

Form 37: Medical Staff Privilege Application Checklist

Objective: *The purpose of this form is to make certain that all of the information required to support an application to the medical staff of a health institution has been sought, has been received and matches the information given by the applicant. Without all information being received, the application cannot move forward to the recommendation or consideration stage. Similarly, if any of the information received does not conform with the requirements necessary for appointment, it cannot be recommended or considered.*

Application: *This form goes into effect when the application is received and has been accepted as an application with all information requested having been provided by the applicant. Failure on the part of the institution to ensure that all criteria necessary for appointment has been provided and is correct, may raise the allegation that the institution has been negligent in appointing a physician who it knew or ought to have known did not meet reasonable standards to carry out procedures applied for in the institution. The form must be completed based on the information provided in the application, and attached to the application. As each step is confirmed, that part of the form is to be completed along with supporting documentation. Each step should be initialled by the person who handled the verification for that item. When the process is completed, the application form, along with this form and all supporting documentation, moves on to the next step for recommendation. Any reply to an inquiry which indicates a disciplinary action, loss of licence, registration or privileges, or any other matter that does not conform to the information provided in the application must be noted on the form and referred to the chair of the recommending committee. The applicant should be advised and asked for an explanation.*

Cross-references: P2.2; F38; F39; F40

(Name of Institution)					
Medical Staff Privilege Application Checklist					
Name of applicant:	(last) (first) (middle)				
Date of application:	_____ / ____ / ____ (yyyy) (mm) (dd)				
Privileges applied for:	_____				
		Date Inquiry Made	Date Response Rec'd	Check ALERT	Sign.
Current Professional Licences	1. ____ 2. ____	____ ____	____ ____	____ ____	____ ____
Previous Licences	1. ____ 2. ____	____ ____	____ ____	____ ____	____ ____
Current or pending disciplinary actions	1. ____ 2. ____	____ ____	____ ____	____ ____	____ ____
Previous disciplinary actions	1. ____ 2. ____	____ ____	____ ____	____ ____	____ ____
Previous medical staff privileges held:	1. ____ 2. ____	____ ____	____ ____	____ ____	____ ____
Education: undergraduate Medical Post-graduate		____ ____ ____	____ ____ ____	____ ____ ____	____ ____ ____

		Date Inquiry Made	Date Response Rec'd	Check ALERT	Sign.
Internship:	_____	_____	_____	_____	_____
Residencies:	1. _____	_____	_____	_____	_____
	2. _____	_____	_____	_____	_____
Specialty qualifications:	1. _____	_____	_____	_____	_____
	2. _____	_____	_____	_____	_____
	3. _____	_____	_____	_____	_____
Criminal background check:	_____	_____	_____	_____	_____
	_____	_____	_____	_____	_____
	_____	_____	_____	_____	_____
Citizenship (If not a Canadian citizen, state status in Canada):	_____	_____	_____	_____	_____
	_____	_____	_____	_____	_____
Awards:	1. _____	_____	_____	_____	_____
	2. _____	_____	_____	_____	_____
Publications:	1. _____	_____	_____	_____	_____
	2. _____	_____	_____	_____	_____
Current malpractice coverage:	_____	_____	_____	_____	_____

Name of Applicant: _____ Page (2/3)

		Date Inquiry Made	Date Response Rec'd	Check ALERT	Sign.
Outstanding items that could not be verified:					

GENERAL STAFF AND OFFICE ADMINISTRATION — Medical Staff Privileges

Form 38: Medical Staff Privileges Application

Objective: *The purpose of this form is not only to commence the process of applying for medical staff privileges in order to treat patients in the institution and to use institutional facilities and supplies and have the support of institutional staff and employees, but also to create a contractual relationship in which the applicant is bound by the rules, regulations and bylaws of the institution in return for receiving specified privileges.*

Application: *This form must be completed by every applicant for medical staff privileges. Once completed and submitted, the medical staff privileges process may commence with a determination finally being made. The second part of the form is completed when this determination has been made, and the form is returned to the applicant.*

Cross-references: P2.2; F37; F39; F40

(Name of Institution)
Medical Staff Privileges Application

I, _____ of (address) _____
hereby apply to (name of institution) _____for
membership in the medical staff and (note class) _____
privileges.

I understand that if, in the discretion of the board of trustees of the (name of institution) _____ I am granted privileges, I hereby agree to be bound by all rules, regulations and bylaws governing the institution and its medical staff, and shall conduct myself within the legal requirements governing the institution and the practice of medicine, and all applicable codes of conduct.

I furthermore agree that I shall maintain absolute confidentiality over all information pertaining to the patients, staff, employees and any matter regarding the administration or operation of the institution.

I understand that I shall not take any action that will be detrimental to the institution nor place me in a position of conflict of interest.

In making this application, I give to the institution and its appointed employees or agents the authority to seek further information on my professional background and any information that will assist in the determination of the granting of privileges.

Signature of applicant:

....

Name of applicant: _____   _____   _____
                          (last)   (first)   (middle)

                   (suffix) Jr., Sr., II, III, etc.: _____

Address: _____   _____

Telephone. _____

Fax: _____   _____

e-mail: _____

1.   Privileges applied for: _____

2.   Current professional licences (attach photocopy):

(jurisdiction) _____

(expiry date) _____

(restrictions) _____

Add additional if any. _____

_____

3.   Previous licences:

(jurisdiction) _____

(expiry date) _____

(restrictions) _____

Add additional if any. _____

4.   Current pending unsettled discipline actions:

Discipline actions	Jurisdictions	Disciplinary body

5.   Previous discipline actions:

Discipline actions	Jurisdictions	Disciplinary body	Dates	Results

6.   Other currently held staff privileges:

Institution	Address

7.   Previous medical staff privileges held:

Institution	Address	Dates held	Status Resigned/removed/disciplined

8.   Education (list undergraduate, professional and post-graduate degrees, institutions, addresses, dates):

Institutions	Address	Degrees	Dates

9.   Internship:

Institutions	Address	Dates

10.   Residencies:

Institutions	Addresses	Specialties	Dates

11.   Specialty qualifications:

Specialty qualifications	Certifying body	Date received

Name of Applicant: _____ Page (3/4)

12. Criminal convictions in Canada or elsewhere (list offence, jurisdiction, date convicted):

Offence	Jurisdiction	Date convicted

13. Citizenship: _____

If not a Canadian citizen, state status in Canada (attach photocopy of documentation)

_____

14. Awards (list with issuing body and dates):

Awards	Issuing Body	Dates

15. Publications:

_____

16. Current malpractice coverage (list insurer or protective society):

_____

17. Past malpractice actions (jurisdiction, date, allegation):

Jurisdictions	Date	Allegation

18. Current malpractice actions pending (jurisdiction, allegation):

Jurisdiction	Allegation

GENERAL STAFF AND OFFICE ADMINISTRATION —
Medical Staff Privileges

Form 39: Medical Staff Reference Verification

Objective: *This form is required as part of the information that must be considered by the recommending committee and the decision-making body on medical staff privileges. To make certain that the information, which is needed to make an informed decision, is obtained this form is designed to encourage the respondent to provide the information that is requested rather than to allow the respondent to respond by means of a letter, which may not address all items requested.*

Application: *This form is to be sent to those institutions named by the applicant for medical staff privileges. It has three parts. The first is the request for information. The second is to be signed by the applicant authorizing the institution to release the information requested, and releasing the institution from any liability that might otherwise be imposed due to the release of the information or arising from the contents of the information or any errors that may have arisen in the contents.*

Cross-references: P2.2; F37; F38; F40

(Name of Institution)

Medical Staff Reference Form

To (name): _____

Institution: _____

Address: _____

_____

Re: Physician _____

Address: _____

_____

The above named physician, Dr. _____ has applied to our institution for medical staff privileges and has given us the name of your institution as a reference in support of the information the applicant has provided to us. In order to assist us in considering the application, we would sincerely appreciate your assistance by completing the form in this request and returning it to us in the self-addressed stamped envelope.

Attached you will find a release signed by the applicant authorizing you to release this information to us.

....

Authorization to release information

I, Dr. _____ of _____
have applied for medical staff privileges at the (name of institution) _____ at (address) _____.

In order to assist in the review of my application, I hereby authorize the release to (name of institution) _____
of any and all information related to my qualifications, practice, conduct and relations related to the period during which I held medical staff privileges, employment or any other position at any other institution to which this request may be sent in support of my application for privileges. Furthermore, I hereby hold harmless any institution providing such information as a result of any errors or omissions in the information provided, exempting gross negligence in providing such information.

(signature) _____

(date) _____

(witness signature) _____

(witness print name) _____

....

Reference regarding medical staff

The following information is taken from our records and is correct to the best of our knowledge.

Dr. _____

Address: _____

Associated with this institution in the following capacities during the dates noted:

    a.   Intern   □ yes □ no   date: from _____ to _____

    b.   Resident □ yes □ no

        Date: from _____ to _____

        Department _____

        Privileges held _____

        Restrictions _____

    c.   Medical staff □ yes □ no

        Date: from _____ to _____

        Department _____

        Privileges held (if altered give dates for each) _____

        Restrictions _____

4.   At any time, was the applicant disciplined? □ yes □ no

    If yes, give dates and reasons.

    _____

    _____

5.   If the applicant failed to renew his position, please give reasons as stated.

    _____

    _____

6.   At any time, was the applicant the subject of a malpractice suit in which the institution was also named as a defendant? □ yes   □ no If yes, give details.

_____

_____

Thank you for your assistance in this matter.

Signature: _____

Title (medical director): _____

GENERAL STAFF AND OFFICE ADMINISTRATION —
Medical Staff Privileges

Form 40: Medical Staff Privileges Granting

Objective: *This form is designed to produce a consistent method of documenting the granting or refusing of medical staff privileges so that any confusion will be removed as to what a physician or surgeon can or cannot do within a hospital. It also ties in with the application so that it is clear that there is a contractual relationship between the physician and the institution.*

Application: *This form is to be delivered by the appropriate administrative officer following a decision having been made in response to the application for medical staff privileges.*

Cross-references: P2.2; F37; F38; F39

(Name of Institution)

Medical Staff Privileges Granting

To: Dr. _____

Address: _____

Re: Medical Staff Privileges Granting

This is to advise that the Board of Trustees of the _____
Hospital duly authorized at its meeting on the ____ day of _____,
20___ and in response to your application for medical staff privileges of
the ____ day of _____ , 20 ____, has granted you membership in the
medical staff of the _____ Hospital for the period commencing _____ and expiring on _____.

You will be assigned to the following department(s):

_____

_____

Your privileges are delineated as follows subject to availability of space
and the ability at the time of the hospital to provide the necessary services:

1.   admission of patients

2.   procedures

3.   assisting in procedures

4.   discharge

It is understood that these privileges are granted subject to the rules,
regulations, bylaws and policies of the hospital. You will be required to
take part in such advisory and supervisory activities, and provide services
on an emergency basis as determined by the head of the department and
other hospital authorities, and to assist in the quality assurance, patient
safety and risk management programs of the hospital. In accepting this
appointment, you agree to meet all ethical standards governing the
hospital and the medical profession, and shall not engage in any activities
that give rise to a conflict of interest.

Administrative officer: _____ (signed)

_____ (print name)

_____ (position)

Date: _____

Acceptance: _____ (signed)

_____ (print name)

_____ (address)

Date: _____

GENERAL STAFF AND OFFICE ADMINISTRATION —
General Safety Issues

Form 41: Physical Inspection of Premises

Objective: *The risk of liability may arise not only from professional practice but from injuries or potential injuries caused by defects in the physical premises of an office, examining room or clinic. It is important that at least twice a year a physical inspection be made to identify conditions that could conceivably give rise to injury of patients, visitors or employees. The purpose of this inspection is to identify risks, and to set in motion a process by which the risks will be removed or at least minimized.*

This form sets up a record to provide evidence that an inspection was made, and that reasonable steps were taken to avoid the risks.

Dates for regular inspections must be placed on the calendar at six-month intervals or even more frequently. Additional inspections should also take place if there is any indication of problems or any change in the premises.

It would be helpful if someone from outside the office took part in the inspection, since those who work in the premises may not consider certain defects as risks because they have become used to them, and may not even notice them as risks.

The inspection must take place when the office is closed so that those inspecting will not be distracted by ordinary office activity. No other activity should be taking place during the inspection.

In doing the inspection, it must be recalled that what is not a risk for someone who ordinarily works there, may be a risk for someone from the outside, especially if the person is impaired, weak or a child. The inspection should take place from this point of view.

So that nothing is missed, the inspection must follow this list exactly. Since the following is a prototypical list, it should be adapted for the particular premises to be inspected.

Application: *This form is to be used by the designated individual responsible for the overall management and physical premises of the practice.*

(Name of Institution)		
Physical Inspection of Premises		

Conducted by: _____

Assisted by: _____

Date: _____

	(check one)	
Item	**Acceptable**	**Repairs Needed**
Parking lot (potholes)		
Parking lot (obstructions)		
Outside steps (holes, insecurities)		
Outside steps (secure hand rails)		
Access for disabled (compatible with wheelchairs)		
Access for disabled (condition)		
Exterior lights (parking lot)		
Exterior lights (walkway)		
Exterior steps		
Exterior disabled ramp		
Interior steps (condition)		
Interior railings		
Flooring (doorway lips)		
Flooring (carpeting)		
Flooring (tiles)		
Flooring (slippery)		
Chairs (secure, no sharp edges or protrusions)		
Occasional tables, desk lamps, other furniture (secure, including for children climbing or adults using for support, no sharp edges or protrusions)		

Examining table (secure, no sharp edges or protrusions) (test in various positions, sections secure)		
Step stools (secure, no sharp edges or protrusions)		
Doorframes (no sharp edges)		
Electrical outlets, wires and plugs (obstruction of passage, injurious to children, no bare wires)		
Physically dangerous items such as sharps, drugs, poisons, cleaning supplies (security from children, the mentally ill or retarded, or dementia patients)		
Blinds and window treatments (secure from falling by anyone who grabs them such as children)		
Doorways leading to restricted areas (secure, signage alone not sufficient for children or visibly or mentally impaired)		
Emergency doors (clearly marked, accessible and can be opened)		
Fire extinguishers (accessible to staff but not others)		
Emergency lighting (tested)		
Accessibility of alarm or emergency bell		

GENERAL STAFF AND OFFICE ADMINISTRATION —
General Safety Issues

Form 42: Group Trips

Objective: *The purpose of this form is to avoid leaving anyone behind in group trips of residents or patients, and leaving anyone on the bus when he or she should have disembarked.*

Application: *This form is to be used by the person in charge of any group tour by bus or other means. It is to be used for groups either from an institution or as part of an organized group such as a day care program.* **One copy of this form is to remain at the facility and one copy by attending staff on the outing.**

(Name of Institution)	
Group Trip Head Count	
One copy of this form is to remain at the facility and one copy by attending staff on the outing.	
Trip Date:	
Transportation (name of bus company, number of bus):	
Driver: Cell no.:	
Supervising attending staff member: Cell no.:	
Names of attendant staff:	(please print) _____
Names of volunteers attending:	(please print) _____ _____ _____
Time of Departure:	
Expected time of return:	
Actual time of return:	

Total number of persons on board the bus (excluding driver):

AT TIME OF BOARDING: (TIME) ____   Location: ____

AT TIME OF FIRST DE-BOARDING: (TIME) ____   Location: ____

AT TIME OF SECOND BOARDING: (TIME) ____   Location: ____

AT TIME OF SECOND DE-BOARDING: (TIME) ____   Location: ____

(add others as necessary)

THE GROUP IS NOT TO LEAVE UNLESS ALL NUMBERS BOARDING AND DEBOARDING ARE THE SAME.

If the counting of participants indicates that someone is missing, the facility shall be notified immediately for instructions and a search shall begin. Records of the details of the efforts made and of the times involved shall be made on this form.

....

Participants List

* Check off the name of each resident who boards the bus initially.
* AND check off the name of each resident each time they disembark and reboard.
* Every time someone gets off the bus and reboards, do a count of the number of people on board. This number MUST equal the number above.
* On return to the facility, CHECK OFF the name of each resident as they disembark to make certain that no one remains on the bus.

Name	Room No.	Boarding (#1)	Boarding (#2)		Return arrival

Form completed by:

GENERAL STAFF AND OFFICE ADMINISTRATION —
General Safety Issues

Form 43: Bomb Threat or Other Threat of Violence

Objective: *The purpose of this form is to record accurately the details of a bomb threat received either by telephone or in writing. Once the threat is received, and recorded, the record of the threat is be given to the security official and the police in order to maintain accuracy, which might otherwise be lost because of time lapse and the influence of a stressful situation, and to maintain consistency among reports given to various officials.*

Application: *This form is to be completed by any person who receive a bomb or other threat of violence against any person whether affiliated with the institution, a patient, or someone not affiliated. It is to be immediately given to the head of security of the institution who shall notify the CEO and the police.*

(Name of Institution)		
Bomb Threat or Other Threat of Violence Report For those questions that are not applicable, mark "N/A"		
Threat:	(check one)	□ telephone □ letter □ fax □ e-mail □ in person
Date received:		
Time:		
Received by:	(print name)	
Location:		
Witnesses to the threat (if applicable):		
Received on telephone number:		
Reported to:	(name) _____ (position) _____ (telephone no.) _____ Time reported: _____	
Information about bomb threat *(receiver to obtain information by asking these questions)*:	When will the bomb explode? _____ _____ (date) (time) Where is the bomb now? _____ Can you describe it? _____ What kind of bomb is it? _____	

What will set it off? _____

_____

Who planted the bomb? _____

_____

Why would anyone want to plant a bomb? ___

_____

In case we are disconnected, may I have a telephone number so I can get back to you?

_____

Do you live near here? Whereabouts? _____

_____

In case I am asked, could you give me your name?

_____

_____

<u>Tone and characteristics of caller's voice</u> (check all that apply):

<u>Also to be completed if threat made in person</u> □ yes □ no

    □Male   □ female

    □ Adult   □ child   □ older adult

    □ Normal (calm)

    □ Angry

    □ Hesitant

    □ Whispered

    □ Raspy

    □ Slurred (as if drunk)

    □ Soft   □ loud

    □ Slow □ fast □ clipped □ stutter □ breathy

    □ Clearing throat □ coughing □ muffled □ lisp

□ Raised voice at end of sentences (almost questioning)

□ Laughter □ giggled

□ Crying   □ hysterical

□ Use of interjections, *e.g.*, "like", crudities or foul language (please note words used)

_____

□ Sound disguised or artificial

□ Accent (check one which might apply)

  □ English (British)

  □ Scottish

  □ Irish

  □ French (European)

  □ French-Canadian

  □ Cape Breton

  □ Newfoundland

  □ Ottawa Valley

  □ New York (Brooklyn, *etc.*)

  □ Boston

  □ Rhode Island

  □ Southern U.S.

  □ African-American

  □ Chinese/Asian

  □ Arabic

  □ Eastern European

  □ Indian/Pakistani

  □ Hispanic

  □ Israeli

☐ Germanic

☐ Italian

☐ Scandinavian

Background sounds (if any) (check all that may apply)

☐ Street noises ☐ cars   ☐ trucks

☐ Machinery ☐ (clear) ☐ (in distance) ___

☐ Muffled

☐ Music: type (describe) _____

☐ Static

☐ Dogs: ☐ bark pitch (describe): _____

☐ Howl _____ more than once

☐ Cat

☐ Voices:

English-speaking (non-accented) _____
English-speaking (accented) (describe) _____

_____

Foreign language _____
— Characteristics (describe) _____
— Language _____

Threat made in person:
•   Name of person
•   ☐ Male ☐ female
•   Description:

Height _____

Weight _____

Build _____

Hair colour _____

Bald _____

Skin colour _____

Complexion _____

Race _____

Type of hair _____

Scars _____

Moles _____

Tattoos _____

Jewelry _____

Beard _____

Mustache _____

Description of lips _____

Glasses ☐ yes ☐ no

    If yes, description: _____

    Description of clothing: _____

Signature of person reporting: _____

Print Name: _____

Date: _____

GENERAL STAFF AND OFFICE ADMINISTRATION — Office Administration

Form 44: Healthcare Message Log

Objective: *While many messages to physicians and healthcare providers are recorded electronically, the reality is that the common practice is still to leave messages by telephone with a receptionist, secretary or other personnel. The well-being of the patient frequently depends on the message being understood, recorded accurately and transmitted accurately. The purpose of this form is to assist in meeting this standard of communication. When the message is given by telephone or in person directly to the individual who is to act on it, this form also assists in lessening the risk of errors and making certain that the person who receives the information is not subject to the uncertainties of lapses in memory.*

Application: *A supply of this form should be maintained at any place where messages may be received, and would be used by anyone receiving telephone messages or messages in person. No more than one message should be placed on each page. The forms should also be printed in duplicate so that one copy is given to the person who is to receive the message, and the other maintained in the appropriate patient's file so that there is a record that a message regarding the patient was received. This form may also be used for calls received from patients.*

(Name of Institution)		
Message Log		
Message for:	(name)	(position)
Urgent:	☐ Yes ☐ No	
Date received:		Time:
Name of caller:		(position)
Received by:		(position)
Name of patient:		
Name of attending physician:		
Message from caller:		
Advice given to caller (if any):		
Message to be delivered to:		
Message delivery attempts:	☐ Delivery made: _____ _____ (date) (time) ☐ Delivery attempted and: _____ _____ (date) (time)	
Follow-up if delivery not made:		
Received by (signature):		

GENERAL STAFF AND OFFICE ADMINISTRATION —
Office Administration

Form 45: Physician's Notice of Absence or Closing of Practice

Objective: *The purpose of this form is to advise the patient that the physician giving the notice will not be available during a particular period, to enable the patient who has a continuing dependence on the physician to make alternative arrangements, and to advise the patient if other arrangements are being made. It is a recognition that there is some responsibility and in many cases a legal duty on the part of the healthcare provider not to abandon the patient, which could cause patient injury. By having written evidence that the provider has taken all reasonable steps to make certain that there is continuity of care, the responsibility then shifts to the patient to take reasonable steps in response.*

Application: *This form must be mailed directly or given to a patient several weeks before the physician is going to be absent. The length of time must be reasonably sufficient to enable the patient to transfer care to another provider. If a particular community does not have someone available, the length of time must be longer so that someone can be found in another community, and assistance provided to enable a provider to be found. This form with the appropriate alterations may also be used for healthcare providers other than physicians, such as dentists, physiothera-pists, psychologists, optometrists, etc.*

Cross-references: P3.4; F6; F11

(Name of Institution)

Physician's Notice of Absence or Closing of Practice

Dear (name of patient or guardian or parent of a minor patient) (choose one):

☐ This is to advise that I will not be available to provide care for my regular patients during the period from _____ to _____.
I have made arrangements for care to be provided during this period by Dr. _____, (address) _____ (telephone) _____.

☐ This is to advise that I will be leaving my practice commencing the (date) _____ and will not be available to provide care for my regular patients after that date. I have made arrangements for care to be provided by Dr. _____, (address) _____ (telephone) _____.

☐ Unfortunately, there are no providers in this community who are able to take additional patients. In consulting with the provincial medical society and the provincial department of health, I have been advised that the nearest providers are as follows:

   (address) _____ (telephone) _____

   (address) _____ (telephone) _____

   (address) _____ (telephone) _____

If you are in agreement with transferring your care to one of these providers, please indicate this by signing this letter and returning it to me. If you wish to have a different provider look after your care, please note this and make certain that the doctor has agreed to accept you as a patient. By indicating your choice, I will accept this as your authorization to make copies of the relevant records in your file and forward them to the provider you have indicated, and to advise that provider on any matter regarding your care that may be necessary.

If you have any questions, please do not hesitate to call my office.

With my many thanks for your understanding and assistance in making these arrangements.

(signature of provider) _____

(print name) _____

(date) _____

....

By signing this document, I hereby authorize to transfer any information from my files to Dr. _____ (address) _____ and to discuss with Dr. _____ any matter concerning my condition for the purpose of taking over my care.

(signature of patient) _____

(print name) _____

(date) _____

INDEX

All References are to Forms and Policies.

NON-ENGLISH SPEAKING PATIENTS, P1.6.3-5, P4.6

ORAL COMMUNICATIONS BY STAFF, P1.6
comprehension of, P1.6.3-6
confidentiality of, P1.6.7
recording of, P1.6.1-2
telephone, by, P1.63-4

PATIENTS
advice sheet, F1
authorization to disclose information, F3
complaints, F36, P7.2
consent to treatment, *see* CONSENT TO TREATMENT
discharge instructions, F8
expectations, P3.2
information, *see* records
missed appointments, F6
property list and release, F4
records, P5.1-5
• advice sheet
• disposal of, P5.5, F1
• forms, completion of, P5.3
• handwritten, P5.2
• handling and maintenance of, standards, P5.1, P5.4
• loss or theft of patient information, F32
• oral communication, P1.6.1.2
• patient information, F2
• patient information, authorization to disclose, F3
• recording of patient information, P5.1
• reports to be received, F26
• retention of, P5.5
• special handling and alerts, F5
• storage of, P5.5
representative, F12
safety
• medical, surgical, other devices, use of, P6.1
• patient test results, loss of or incorrect, F33
• physical safety of premises, F41
temporary absence from healthcare provider, F9

PERSONAL CONDUCT, P1.3.3

PHOTOGRAPHS, CONSENT TO, P8.1.11, F25

PHYSICAL CONTACT
among staff, P1.4.3
between staff and patients, P3.3
between volunteers, staff and patients, P2.3.7

PREMISES, PHYSICAL INSPECTION OF, F41

PRESS
attendance at meetings, *see* MEETINGS, access to press and public
statements, *see* PUBLIC STATEMENTS

PUBLIC STATEMENTS, P1.2.2, P2.3.13, P8.1

REFERRALS AND CONSULTATIONS, P3.5
request for, P3.5.1
tracking, P3.5.2

REFUSAL OF TREATMENT (CONSENT), P4.3, F17

REPORTS TO BE RECEIVED, F26

REPRESENTATIVE OF PATIENT, F12

RESEARCH PROCEDURES, P4.7

RESEARCHER'S PLEDGE OF CONFIDENTIALITY, F34

RESTRAINT, PHYSICAL, P1.3.3

RETENTION OF PATIENT RECORDS, P5.5

RISK MANAGEMENT, *see* UNEXPECTED OUTCOME

RULES OF ORDER, *see* MEETINGS, procedure and rules of order

SAFETY OF PATIENT, *see* PATIENTS, safety

SALUTATION, P1.4.2